DESIGNED FOR PURPOSE
WOMAN, FEARFULLY AND WONDERFULLY MADE...

JENNIFER WALLACE

NOBRICH

Published by:
NOBRICH
P. O. Box 38737
London
E17 5WZ
United Kingdom

Another Book by Jennifer Wallace
 FREE TO SERVE, God's Liberated Woman

ISBN: 978-0-9558369-0-9

Distributed by NOBRICH
Tel: +44 (0)7958 809874
Email: Nobrich@aol.com

Cover Design and typeset by Antony Norris
Email: antony@project10.com

DEDICATION

To Nobelle,
The Fruit of My Womb

CONTENTS

Page

PREFACE

I originally intended dealing with this topic as a chapter in another book, which God-willing, I will be writing later. However, I felt the Holy Spirit prompting me to write a separate book on the topic, as there is an urgent need for women to discover the nature of God in them and their God-given strengths. This will empower and enable them to rise up and effectively be used by God.

Infact, when the Lord prompted me to write this book, I had just come back from a hectic mission trip to Nigeria, Cameroon and Ghana. Moreover, He also gave me a timeframe of about four months to write and publish it! I was very tired and had a pile of work to attend to, as well as taking care of my family, and so I promised Him I would write after I had sorted things out and rested. Actually, I had every reason not to write immediately and so did not make writing this book a priority.

However, God has His own ways of getting things done! Shortly after I came home from that mission trip, I developed a sore-throat and lost my voice, which persisted for almost two months. My dear friend Barbara advised me to go and see my doctor who prescribed antibiotics and instructed me not to speak for two weeks! The medication made me feel very ill and so I had to spend my time in bed. Feeling very miserable and low, I asked Father God, *"How did I get to this place?"* He began to impress on my heart the need to write this book. My excuse in the past had been that I was busy, tired and overworked, but, here I was, in bed, bored, unable to speak and do much work.

However, I was still not convinced about the book, especially since two months had already gone by, until I received a text message from my friend Lucille saying, and I quote, *"Hang in there, you fighter! It will NOT be for long! I bet there'll be a book at the end of your vocal time-out. Stay focused on God's grace."* Immediately, I knew what to do…!

I am grateful for the opportunity to write this book, as it has brought great joy to me. It is, therefore, my prayer that many will be blessed by it.

Jennifer Wallace
A Woman in Tune, Listening & Obeying

Acknowledgements

- To God, my Father, for entrusting me with such a great responsibility and supplying grace to deliver this book on time.
- To my dear husband Cobby and my two great children, Nobelle and Richard, for bearing up with me and enduring the text messages and phone calls from my bedroom.
- To Barbara Hills, for caring enough to prompt me to go to my doctor, and bringing a sense of direction to my life once again.
- To Barbra Simpson, Jackie Magloire, Hyacinth Morris and Margaret Fordjuor for your encouragement, support and proof-reading at such short notice.
- To Lucille Onyema for being in-tune, once again, and sending me that text…
- To Jacqui Peart, thanks for all your advice.
- To Antony Norris, a 'gift from God'. Thank you for helping me out with all your skills, talents, equipments and contacts.
- Finally, but not the least, to all the women in my February 2008 Mentoring Class, for your support, encouragement and prayers.

May God richly bless you all.

INTRODUCTION

"For You formed my inward parts; You wove me in my mother's womb. I will give thanks to You, for I am fearfully and wonderfully made; Wonderful are Your works, and my soul knows it very well." – Psalm 139:13-14 (NASB)

The subject matter of this book has been an issue of interest to me for a long time. I vividly remember growing up as young girl, carefree and uninhibited. I could come out of the bathroom naked and unashamed; dancing, singing or shivering, yes, but never ashamed. Then, somehow, things suddenly changed! It was no longer appropriate for me come out of the bathroom in my birthday suit – I was simply told to cover up. That was when I began to gain more awareness about my body, and also, feel shame.

The truth is, I had just entered into puberty and it was no longer appropriate for others, especially men, to see my bare body as there were major changes taking place. My body was rapidly developing and I was being transformed from a girl into a woman. As beautiful as my body was becoming, the constant admonishment to 'cover up' created shame, rather than pride and appreciation. This, unfortunately, made me miss the initial and important lessons God would teach me about myself and His creation called "WOMAN."

I have, however, discovered with time that this experience is not peculiar to me, but has been the dilemma of women in most cultures for ages. The prescribed shame and lack of appreciation for the female body, except perhaps, for sexual purposes, has caused us to miss the many vital strengths God has set within our blueprint. Hence, many women are not only ashamed of their bodies, but also consider themselves weak. Thank God, for another chance to discover how we have been fearfully and wonderfully created in His image.

Romans 1:20

"For since the creation of the world His invisible attributes are clearly seen, being understood by the things that are made, even His eternal power and Godhead"

The attributes of God are manifested in the physical; hence our physiology should tell us something about ourselves, and the nature of God in us. God's nature is entwined into every facet of our being; therefore, a study of the physical make-up of woman should give us more insight and understanding of our spiritual make-up. Therefore, the purpose of this book is not to debate or make comparisons between men and women, but to stir up women to discover and appreciate their God-given gifts, which are manifested in their body.

So, to all the women who read this book, I hope and pray that it succeeds in what it set out to do, that is, enlighten, equip and empower you. For all the men, I hope and pray that this book serves as an eye-opener and causes you to understand and appreciate the essential qualities women possess, which the Body of Christ needs now, more than ever. God bless.

Jennifer Wallace
A Woman in Tune, Listening and Obeying

Chapter One

MOTHER OF ALL LIVING

A Tragic Beginning

The Garden of Eden was more quiet than usual, as the Lord God descended from on high to enjoy the beauty of creation and have fellowship with man and woman, whom He had made in His perfect image. Yet, there was something eerie about the silence, enhanced by the darkened sun. The trees bowed their heads, the mountains quaked in anger and fear, and the sea roared in anguish. The rivers began to recoil, shrivelling at the sound of God's footsteps. No, something was very wrong!

Suddenly, a deer raced by, with a roaring lion at its heels, desperate to catch and devour it. All the other animals were at each others throats, with the weak fleeing from the strong and the small hiding from the large. There was chaos, once again, on God's beautiful earth, which He had entrusted to Man to subdue, dominate and occupy. However, Man was nowhere to be found!

God knew that something terrible had happened to His beautiful creation! Of course, He had watched it happen, but could do nothing about it, because to determine how loyal Man would remain to His maker, He had given them a will.

"Where are you?" The Lord God called out to Adam

Both the man and the woman crept from behind a rock, looking awkward and pitiful in what looked like fig-leaves skirts. The man replied, *"We heard Your footsteps in the garden, and were afraid and hid ourselves because we were naked."*

"Who told you that you were naked? Have you eaten of the tree of which I commanded you that you should not eat?" God asked, even though He already knew the answer.

"The woman whom You gave to be with me gave me some fruit from the tree, and I ate," the man replied, trying to ignore the woman's glaring looks.

The Lord God turned to the woman, *"What is this you have done?"*

"The serpent cheated, outwitted, and deceived me, and I ate," the woman said, as she tried to adjust her fig-leaf skirt with one hand and cover her breasts with the other.

In fury, the Lord God announced to the serpent, as there was no point in asking him what he had done, *"Because you have done this, you are cursed above all animals and above every living thing of the field. From now on you shall crawl on your belly and eat dust and its contents, all the days of your life."*

The smile on the serpent's face vanished as He contemplated God's words and their effect on him forever. But God hadn't finished with him yet,

"I, the Lord God, will make the woman your worse enemy, and she will make you pay for what you have done. I will also put enmity between your offspring and her Offspring, Who will bruise and tread your head underfoot, as you lie in wait to bruise His heel."

The serpent crawled angrily away, already plotting his next move. As they watched his slithering body move slowly in the dust, God turned again to the woman and said,

"I have no choice than to punish you, for my justice will not permit me to ignore this. I will greatly multiply your grief and your suffering in pregnancy and childbearing; with spasms of distress you will bring forth children. Yet your desire and craving will be for your husband, and he will rule over you."

Both the woman and man were stunned by what God had just said! *"No!"* The woman cried, as the man quivered in fear and grim anticipation. The Lord God paused for a while, the anguish in His face was unbearable to behold. Finally, He said to the man,

"Because you have listened and heeded to the voice of your wife and have eaten of the tree of which I commanded you not to, the ground is cursed because of you. In sorrow and toil shall you eat of its fruits all the days of your life. The earth shall also bring forth thorns and thistle for you and you shall eat the plants of the field. In the sweat of your face you shall

eat bread until you return to the ground, from which you were taken; for dust you are and to dust you shall return!"

The man's shoulders slumped! His knees buckled and dropped to the ground, as the magnitude of his predicament sank in. The situation was dire and there was no turning back! Words failed him and loneliness, shame and sorrow filled his heart, as he pondered over what God's words meant...

"But hang on a minute, what was it God had said to the serpent," the man tried to recollect. *"Something to do with the woman and her Offspring,"* he called to memory, his eyes beginning to see a ray of hope, *"The solution lies with the woman! She will turn things round for humanity when she gives birth! Despite the predicted pain and suffering in childbirth, the fruit of her womb shall save the day!"*

The man's anger towards his wife began to wane. Still kneeling, he raised his head and hands and called out to her, *'Chavvah'* meaning, *'Eve'* or *'Life-Spring'*. The merciful God had declared hope in His judgement. Through the woman and her Offspring, Man shall live again and recover all that was lost. Yes, the woman had been declared the life-spring of humanity, one who nurtures life, the MOTHER OF ALL THE LIVING.[1]

The Offspring of Woman

What was it that prompted Adam to change the woman's name from "Woman"[2] to "Chavvah" (Eve)? What did Adam hear that brought hope and prompted him to declare the woman as the life-spring of humanity? Exactly what did God mean by what He said?

Woman's Offspring would bruise the heel of the enemy. Redemption, deliverance and salvation would come through Him. Jesus Christ, the Messiah, the Seed of woman fulfilled that prophecy by coming to earth, born of a virgin woman and dying on a cross. Through His death and resurrection, every pronunciation against humanity has been cancelled, if we will only believe.

Colossians 2:13-13

"And you, being dead in your trespasses and the uncircumcision of your flesh, He has made alive together with Him, having forgiven you all trespasses, having wiped out the handwriting of requirements that was against us, which was contrary to us. And He has taken it out of the way, having nailed it to the cross. Having disarmed principalities and powers, He made a public spectacle of them, triumphing over them in it"

However, the battle may be over but the war still goes on. The battle has been unquestionably won and victory declared, but the war to take back territory, to reclaim all that was lost and restore Man's rightful position and God's kingdom glory on earth continues. God's promises are sure and must be fulfilled, just as they were fulfilled in the lives of the Israelites.

Joshua 21:43-45

"So the LORD gave Israel all the land He had sworn to give their forefathers, and they took possession of it and settled there. The LORD gave them rest on every side, just as He had sworn to their forefathers. Not one of their enemies withstood them; the LORD handed all their enemies over to them. Not one of all the LORD's good promises to the house of Israel failed; every one was fulfilled."(NIV)

Jesus Christ has won the victory and restored humanity. Whilst He was alive, Jesus called His twelve disciples, gave them power and authority over all demons and diseases, and sent them to preach the kingdom of God and to heal the sick.[3] Before He returned to heaven Jesus gave authority to His disciples, including us.

Mark 16:15-18

"And He said to them, "Go into all the world and preach the gospel to every creature. He who believes and is baptized will be saved; but he who does not believe will be condemned. And these signs will follow those who believe: In My name they will cast out demons; they will speak with new tongues; they will take up serpents; and if they drink anything deadly, it will by no means hurt them; they will lay hands on the sick, and they will recover."

Like David, God has given the Church the power and authority to recover what humanity lost.[4] We must pursue the enemy and recover all, and establish God's rule and reign on earth through Man.

The Life-Spring of Humanity

In order to fulfil the promise of full recovery and restoration, woman, the life-spring of humanity needs to arise and take her place. What qualities did Eve possess for God to put such a huge responsibility on her shoulders? What did God know about Eve, which Adam only recognised after God had spoken?

These are things I am sure you would like to know. What is it in woman, which will turn the world back, right side up? One of my favourite quotations is by Sojourner Truth, an African American woman who lived during the period of slavery:

"If the first woman God ever made was strong enough to turn the world upside down all alone, these women together ought to be able to turn it back, and get it right side up again! And now they is asking to do it, the men better let them."[5]

Please come with me on this journey of discovery and, together, we will find out more about woman, the Life-Spring of Humanity. Let us explore what God put in woman when He created her, which is needed to complete the work of establishing God's kingdom and Christ's rule and reign on earth. Let us discover the essential qualities, attributes and truths about WOMAN, the MOTHER OF ALL LIVING

REFLECTION QUESTIONS

1. Think about the judgement God pronounced to the woman. Can you identify the effects of that judgement in your life

2. Ponder over the serpent's judgement. How do you think that judgement has been executed?

3. Consider God's declaration of enmity between the devil and woman. Do you think that has been fulfilled? If not, how do you think it could be fulfilled?

4. What does 'Mother of all Living' mean to you?

Notes

1. Genesis Chapter 3
2. Genesis 2:23
3. Luke 9:1-2
4. 1 Samuel 30:8-20
5. Sojourner Truth, "Ain't I A Woman", (Speech delivered Dec1851 at Women's Convention, Akron, Ohio), Modern History Sourcebook, Source Online: http://www.fordham.edu/halsall/mod/sojtruth-woman.htm

PURPOSE DETERMINES DESIGN

"The purpose of a thing determines its nature, its design and its features"
– Dr. Myles Monroe.[1]

"The One Flaw in Woman"

My friend Barbara recently sent me an email about the creation of woman, entitled, "The One Flaw in Woman." I went the on internet to find out more about this story, which appears to have been circulating in cyberspace for a while. Unfortunately no one seems to know where it originated from, but it captures the essence of this chapter and book.

It goes like this…

"…By the time the Lord made woman, He was into His sixth day of working overtime. An angel appeared and said, *"Why are you spending so much time on this one?"*

And the Lord answered, *"Have you seen my spec sheet on her? She has to be completely washable, but not plastic, have over 200 movable parts, all replaceable, and able to run on diet Coke and leftovers, have a lap that can hold four children at one time, have a kiss that can cure anything from a scraped knee to a broken heart—and she will do everything with only two hands."*

The angel was astounded at the requirements. *"Only two hands? No way! And that's just on the standard model? That's too much work for one day. Wait until tomorrow to finish."*

"But I won't," the Lord protested. *"I am so close to finishing this creation that is so close to my own heart. She already heals herself when she is sick AND can work 18-hour days."*

The angel moved closer and touched the woman. *"But you have made her so soft, Lord."* *"She is soft,"* the Lord agreed, *"but I have also made her tough. You have no idea what she can endure or accomplish."*

"Will she be able to think?" asked the angel.

The Lord replied, *"Not only will she be able to think, she will be able to reason and negotiate."*

The angel then noticed something, and, reaching out, touched the woman's cheek. *"Oops, it looks like you have a leak in this model. I told you that you were trying to put too much into this one."*

"That's not a leak," the Lord corrected, *"that's a tear!"*

"What's the tear for?" the angel asked.

"The Lord said, *'The tear is her way of expressing her joy, her sorrow, her pain, her disappointment, her love, her loneliness, her grief and her pride."*

The angel was impressed. *"You are a genius, Lord. You thought of everything! Woman is truly amazing."*

And she is! Women have strengths that amaze men. They bear hardships, and they carry burdens; but they hold happiness, love and joy. They smile when they want to scream. They sing when they want to cry. They cry when they are happy and laugh when they are nervous.

They fight for what they believe in. They stand up to injustice. They don't take no for an answer when they believe there is a better solution. They go without so that their family can have. They go to the doctor with a frightened friend. They love unconditionally.

They cry when their children excel and cheer when their friends get awards. They are happy when they hear about a birth or a wedding. Their hearts break when a friend dies. They grieve at the loss of a family member, yet they are strong when they think there is no strength left. They know that a hug and a kiss can heal a broken heart.

Women come in all shapes, sizes and colours. They'll drive, fly, walk, run, or e-mail you this to show how much they care about you. The heart of a woman is what makes the world keep turning. They bring joy, hope and love. They have compassion and ideals. They give moral support to their family and friends. Women have vital things to say and everything to give.

However, if there is one flaw in women, it is that they forget their worth!"[2]

A God of Purpose

How very true and accurate! Whoever wrote this story hit the nail on the head! God had a definite purpose for creating woman. The bible clearly states that God is a God of purpose. Everything He created had a purpose, and there was nothing created that God did not have a motive or reason for. The mountains, hills, rivers, trees and plants all have a purpose. The sun, the moon, etc, all have a purpose. The animals, birds and fishes have a purpose, although I have often wondered what God's original purpose for mosquitoes, mice and cockroaches is!

Colossians 1:16

"For everything, absolutely everything, above and below, visible and invisible ...everything got started in Him and finds its purpose in Him" (TM)

Psalm 33:11

"But the plans of the LORD stand firm forever, the purposes of His heart through all generations." (NIV)

Isaiah 14:24, 26-27

The LORD of hosts has sworn, saying, "Surely, as I have thought, so it shall come to pass, and as I have purposed, so it shall stand... This is the purpose that is purposed against the whole earth, and this is the hand that is stretched out over all the nations. For the LORD of hosts has purposed, and who will annul it? His hand is stretched out, and who will turn it back?"

The Lord also said to the prophet Jeremiah, "Before I formed you in the womb I knew you; before you were born I sanctified you; I ordained you a prophet to the nations."[3] God is a God of purpose. Everything God does has purpose, which is the soul and life of all the laws of order in creation. God does not work in a mindless vacuum; His purposes are firm, established and unchangeable.

The thesaurus defines purpose as the *"reason for which something is done or for which something exists."* Purpose is also defined as *"Motive, motivation, grounds, cause, reason, basis and justification"*[4]

Therefore, God had a motive and reason for creating woman. Rick Warren says, *"The purpose of your life is far greater than your own personal fulfilment, your peace of mind, or even your happiness. It is far greater than your family, your career, or even your wildest dreams or ambitions."*[5] This is because the purpose for life is determined and given by God, and is the only reason for creation and existence.

To have purpose means to have a reason for existence, and there is certainly a reason why woman came into existence. Woman was created in accordance with God's purpose for her. God had a desired effect and outcome in mind when He created woman.

If you don't know the purpose, identity and function of a thing you misuse, abuse, devalue or destroy it.[6] Recently, I was watching "Antiques Road Show", a television programme where people took in objects from their homes to be examined and valued. That particular series featured a woman with a bronze sculpture. She only attended the "Antiques Road Show" out of curiosity and to be featured on television. One of the experts examined the sculpture and discovered it to be a very valuable and expensive one from the 18th century, which was worth thousands of pounds. The woman was very shocked because she had been using the sculpture as a doorstopper at home. She was ignorant of its worth, hence, she had devalued, misused and abused it. Unfortunately, this has been the dilemma of women for centuries.

Purpose, Design and Function

The purpose of a thing determines its design, which also determines its function. For example, if I purposed to create something to sit on when I am tired of standing, I would design and build something with sturdy and strong legs, a flat surface and a back. For argument's sake, let's call my creation a 'chair', and this is how it would function – the flat surface would support my backside and take the weight off my legs, the strong and sturdy legs would ensure the flat surface is well supported and protect my backside from the pull of gravity, and the back of my 'chair' would support my back so that I don't tilt or fall over. When I sat on my 'chair' I would not fall down or break my back, but would be well supported and rested, because my chair had been designed and built to function according to purpose.

This principle of 'purpose, design and function' also applies to the creation of woman. This is because God had a definite purpose for creating woman; hence she was designed to function in a specific and particular manner to enable her to fulfil that purpose.

The Purpose of Woman

Genesis 1:26-27

God spoke: "Let us make human beings in our image, make them reflecting our nature so they can be responsible for the fish in the sea, the birds in the air, the cattle, and, yes, Earth itself, and every animal that moves on the face of Earth." God created human beings; he created them godlike, reflecting God's nature. He created them male and female. God blessed them: "Prosper! Reproduce! Fill Earth! Take charge! Be responsible for fish in the sea and birds in the air, for every living thing that moves on the face of Earth." (TM)

In the beginning, God created Man in His image. To reflect His true image, God created Man as male and female. Man and woman, therefore, were created in God's image to fulfil a two-fold purpose of relationship (based on love) and work. The horizontal functioning between the man and woman in marriage would not only reflect what exists in the Trinity, but also the vertical one of man's worship and service to God. In service, they would rule the earth and take charge by dominating it. In relationship, they would love and support each other and produce fruit (offspring) who would reflect God's image on earth.

Yet, for a while, man was alone and, alas, there was no suitable companion in all of creation for him. God knew this was not good and would not advance His plans and purposes, so He created woman. One reason for this is that for man to truly reflect God's nature, he had to give out love in relationship, but there was no one suitable for him. There was also no one available who had the capacity, ability and capability to reproduce man's seed. Hence, God created woman, who would receive man's love, take his seed, multiply it, bear fruit and replenish the earth. She would also assist man in taking dominion over the earth. In effect, the creation of woman was a direct response to both a need in man and a pursuit of purpose.

God designed and created woman to function and fulfil her purpose. She was designed to receive, multiply, reproduce, nurture and give life. God designed and gave her the capacity to function as He had ordained. Everything about the woman pointed to that purpose. To understand and discover this is to put value and worth on woman once again.

REFLECTION QUESTIONS

1. Review the concept of purpose, design and function. Can you give examples that illustrate the concept?
2. If the purpose of a thing determines its design, what do you

think is the purpose of woman?

3. Ponder again over what you think the purpose of woman is. How does that reflect God's image in you?

4. Prayerfully consider what must change in your thinking and understanding.

Notes

1. Dr. Myles Monroe, "Understanding the Purpose and Power of a Woman", Whitaker House, Pa, 2001, p.134 – 135
2. Unfortunately, there is no known author of this wonderful story. Whoever she is (I suppose it was written by a woman), I salute her!
3. Jeremiah 1:4-5
4. The Merriam-Webster Thesaurus, 1978
5. Rick Warren, 'The Purpose Driven Life' Zondervan, 2002, p.17
6. Proverbs 29:18

Chapter Three

EQUAL BUT DIFFERENT

*"Our sexuality penetrates to the deepest metaphysical ground
of our personality. As a result, the physical differences
between the man and the woman are a parable of the
psychical and spiritual difference of a more ultimate nature"*
– Emil Brunner

It's a Man Thing

Jay was out driving and found herself in unfamiliar surroundings, and so she stopped at a petrol station to ask for directions. Her husband Michael, however, considered this to be a sign of weakness, *"because men never stop and ask for directions"*. Infact, most men would rather drive in a circle for hours, than stop and ask for direction. *"Looks like I've found a new way to get there"*, a man would say, to explain why he's been going round in circles and he's taken longer to arrive at his destination.

My beloved husband Cobby is no exception. If you have ever walked or driven around the West End in London, you would realize it's a real maze! Whenever he tells me he's taking me to the West End, I say to him, *"Can you please find out exactly where the theatre, cinema or restaurant is, because I don't want to walk round in circles."* He always assures me that he knows exactly where we are going, but, guess what, we always end up driving or walking in circles, until I insist we stop and ask for directions, or eventually we arrive at our destination.

This is just one of the perceived differences between men and women. Believe me, it is not a sign of weakness or stupidity on the part of men. It's just a man thing, you know!

'The Amoeba Concept'

Men and women are different. Yes, I hear you, loud and clear, *"In Christ there is neither male nor female, we are all the same"*.[1] I describe this as a kind of 'amoeba concept', where we are all of the same sex, or perhaps, sexless.

I once listened to a radio phone-in programme on the differences between men and women. Almost every caller emphasized that men and women were the same, and refused to acknowledge the differences, constantly making reference to the above scripture. I totally agree with the word of God that in Christ there is neither Greek, Jew, slave or free, male or female.

However, the idea of sameness in this scripture relates more to our relationship with and service to God. The bible describes us all, both men and women, as heirs[2] and sons[3] of God, which is to do with our status, position and responsibility in God through Christ, and highlights our equality rather than our differences. No one can, therefore, dispute the fact that men and women are different.

Just Different

In the beginning, God created man and woman equal but different. Because of their individual purpose and function at creation, God designed and created them differently. The difference in purpose and function explains the apparent biological, psychological and physiological differences between men and women. You only have to take a glance at a man and woman to know they are different. Even men who cross-dress as women are easy to spot because their behaviour and mannerism gives them up. Men and women think, act and behave differently. Men and women see, understand and perceive differently. This is what makes life so interesting, just the way God created it to be.

I must say that I have no intention of writing an in-depth description of the essential differences between men and women in this book, as I am assured there are many books and articles out there on the subject. However, for clarity, I would like us to take a brief look at some of these essential differences, because acknowledging them could help us discover our essential purpose.

Some Differences between Men and Women

Biologists, anatomists, physiologists, psychologist or any other scientist would agree with Emil Brunner (quoted above) and inform you that the differences between men and women are not merely physical, but of a deeper nature. Dr. James Dobson, a renowned Christian psychologist and the founder of Focus on the Family, mentioned some of these differences in his book, "Dr Dobson Answers Your Questions," a few of which have been adapted below.[4]

1. The cells in the bodies of men and women are different. The difference in the chromosome combination (XY for men and XX for women) is the basic cause of development into maleness and femaleness.

2. Due to the difference in chromosome combination, women have greater constitutional vitality than men. This means that, generally, women outlive men by three to four years. *Vive la difference!*

3. The skeletal structure of women is different from men. Women, generally, have shorter heads, broader faces (that is meant to enhance beauty), shorter legs and longer trunks. Men tend to have the opposite.

4. Women have more hair on the head and lesser on the body than men. Again, this enhances beauty, as the bible says, the woman's hair is her covering and glory.[5] However, hair on a woman's body is unseemly and women will go to great lengths to get rid of it.

5. Women have slower metabolism, which is a contributory factor to the easiness with which we gain weight. Now we know why…!

6. There is an obvious and remarkable difference between man and woman in the sizes of various organs. Women have larger stomach, kidneys, liver, and appendix (a necessary requirement to carry another life within the

womb). However, women have smaller lungs, because the other organs occupy more space, I suppose.

7. The thyroid gland is also larger and more active in women. This is associated with smooth skin in women, relatively hairless body and subcutaneous fat, which are important elements in the concept of personal beauty. The Thyroid gland also contributes to emotional instability in women, which causes them to laugh and cry more easily.

8. Women's blood contains more water and, therefore, fewer red blood cells than men's. Since red blood cells carry oxygen to the body, the reduction causes women to tire more easily and be prone to fainting. This is not a sign of weakness in women, but a real biological difference from men.

9. In brute strength men are 50% above women. Yeah!

10. Women have several very important functions totally lacking in men – menstruation, pregnancy and lactation. She also has different hormones from men. All these influence behaviour and feelings.

11. The female brain is wired differently from the male brain. This is a bit scientific and technical, but here it goes: the *hypothalamus*, which is located at the base of the brain, and is often called the 'seat of the emotions,' is apparently wired differently between men and women. For the woman,

a severe emotional shock/trauma can be interpreted by the *hypothalamus*, which then sends messages to the *pituitary gland*. The *pituitary gland* responds by changing the biochemistry of the woman. This can cause changes in her menstrual cycle, hair loss, moods etc. However, this also prepares her body during pregnancy. More of this later...

In his book, "Straight Talk to Men and their Wives", Dr. James Dobson also said that, *"The Female physiology is a finely tuned instrument, being more complex and vulnerable than the male counterpart."*[6] As an expert, he would know, wouldn't he? It is very obvious that God designed and created woman with much attention to every intricate detail, everything in its rightful place and functioning according to purpose.

A van and a sports car are both vehicles, yet they are designed to function differently. They both perform the basic functions of transportation; however, because of their different purposes, they have different designs and functions. The purpose of the van is to transport goods and so it has been functionally designed to carry and transport goods. However, when designing a sports car, the manufacturer will have speed, status and style on his mind, and not goods or freight. The sports car, therefore, will be fast, sleek, flashy and trendy, almost like a status symbol.

The same applies to man and woman. The differences in build, make-up and design were a deliberate act on the part of the 'Manufacturer' (God), because of the difference in purpose. If woman was designed more complex and vulnerable than man, it is because that was what God required to enable her to function according to His intended purpose.

It is interesting to note, however, that the major differences between man and woman are associated with reproduction, which we will discuss in-depth in Chapter 5. Meanwhile, enjoy the differences...!

REFLECTION QUESTIONS

1. Ponder over the phrase, "equal but different." What does that mean to you?
2. Review the list of differences between men and women. Can you add a few of your own?
3. Ask a few men and women what they think the differences between men and women are, and compare their answers. Does that tell you more about the differences between men and women?
4. Discuss how you think women can enjoy the differences between men and women.

Notes

1. Galatians 3:28
2. Galatians 3:29
3. Galatians 4:4-6
4. Adapted from: Dobson, James, "Dr Dobson Answers Your Questions", Kingsway Publications, Eastbourne, UK, 1983, pg 410
5. 1 Corinthians 11:15
6. Dobson, James, "Straight Talk to Men and their Wives" (Waco: Word Books, 1980)

Chapter Four

FEARFULLY AND WONDERFULLY MADE IN THE IMAGE OF GOD

"I will give thanks to You, for I am fearfully and wonderfully made; wonderful are Your works, and my soul knows it very well. My frame was not hidden from You, when I was made in secret, and skilfully wrought in the depths of the earth; Your eyes have seen my unformed substance; and in Your book were all written the days that were ordained for me, when as yet there was not one of them." – Psalm 139:14-16

"My, You Do Look Like Me!"

The witty evangelist, Jesse Duplantis narrated a story about a bulldog he came across somewhere. Jesse said the dog turned its head towards him as if to say, *"My, you do look like me!"* Now, that is an example of someone who bears the image of another!

Seriously, we have been uniquely, fearfully and wonderfully made in God's image.

Genesis 5:1-2

"...In the day that God created man, He made him in the likeness of God. He created them male and female, and blessed them and called them Mankind in the day they were created

Man (generic) was created in the image of God as male and female. This indicates that individually, man and woman would reflect aspects of God, and together, they would reflect the total image and essence of God on earth. This is an unchangeable truth, which no one can alter. Therefore, Man, created as male and female in God's image, would reflect the distinct aspects of the divine glory on earth. This means that man and woman would equally reflect:

1. God's nature, that is, His essential characteristics of love, kindness, patience, mercy and goodness and justice.
2. God's constitution, which is not physical but rather of the soul. This implies that man and woman would possess understanding, will and active power.
3. God's authority, which was manifested in the mandate and authority given to both of them to subdue and take dominion over the earth and everything on it.
4. God's purity and righteousness, having a right standing with Him, in the absence of sin. They would walk in purity and obedience before God.
5. God's function, as demonstrated in the operation within the Trinity, and in the relationship between God the Father, God the Son and God the Holy Spirit.

This further clarifies that woman was created in God's image as equal to man. However, like Jesus, our equality with men is not a thing to be grasped, but with the same sense of humility, we pursue our purpose, position and status in Christ.[1]

Fearfully and Wonderfully Made

Now, our God is an awesome and wonderful God. Infact, Wonderful is one of the names ascribed to Jesus by the prophet Isaiah.[2] The bible narrates an incident where God asked Moses to bring the people of Israel to Mount Sinai, and there He would manifest and demonstrate His awesome power and glory. When Israel arrived at Sinai, the sight and sound of God's presence on the mountain was so awesome that the people trembled.

Exodus 19:16, 18

"Then it came to pass on the third day, in the morning, that there were thunderings and lightnings, and a thick cloud on the mountain; and the sound of the trumpet was very loud, so that all the people who were in the camp trembled... Now Mount Sinai was completely in smoke, because the LORD descended upon it in fire. Its smoke ascended like the smoke of a furnace, and the whole mountain quaked greatly."

Ezekiel saw the glory of God and was full of awe. David wrote numerous psalms, in an attempt to describe the wonder, majesty, greatness and power of God. Moses, Isaiah, Solomon, John the Apostle – the list is endless – all wrote about the beauty, glory and splendour of God. Just scan through the bible, from Genesis to Revelations, and you will discover awesome truths about God. It is no wonder that David declared in Psalm 139 that he had been *'fearfully and wonderfully'* made. Man and woman have been wonderfully and awesomely made because they were created in the image of an awesome and wonderful God.

37

If you turn to the back cover of this book you will see a photograph, which is a reflection or image of me. For those who know me, there will be no question in your minds that the photo is a true representation of Jennifer Wallace. However, for those who have never met me, you now have an idea of what I look like and may recognise me if you see me in future, because that photograph is my true image.

This brings to mind an incident that occurred a couple of years ago in The Republic of Benin, West Africa. A woman walked up to me and said, *"I almost did not recognise you because I was expecting someone with short hair."* I laughed, because the flyers had a photograph of me with short hair, but being a normal woman, I had changed my hairstyle since that photograph was taken. I found it interesting that the woman had formed an idea of what I looked like, based on the picture (image, copy or reflection) of me.

As women, we possess God's awesome and wonderful nature. We have been uniquely, fearfully and wonderfully made in His image. God deposited aspects of His nature and power in us at creation. Unfortunately, that power is latent and remains untapped. We need to begin to realise who we really are and what we are capable of doing in Christ.

Romans 1:20

"For since the creation of the world His invisible attributes are clearly seen, being understood by the things that are made, even His eternal power and Godhead..."

God's nature is entwined with every facet of our being and physique. The above scripture tells us that the invisible attributes of God are manifested in the things that we see, hence a good look at the female body must tell us about the awesome and fearful nature of God in us.

Unfortunately, many of us find it difficult to look at our physical bodies. As said earlier, this is an acquired shame that has been imposed on us since childhood. This acquired shame hinders us from appreciating our physical body and learning from it. Woman, your body is a gift from God, so appreciate and love it, and discover your inherent and God-given strengths and attributes. Studying the physical make-up of woman will give us more insight and understanding into our spiritual make-up.

Reproducing After Kind

As said in the previous chapter, the most profound differences between men and women are linked to reproduction. This is because part of God's mandate to Man was to be fruitful and multiply and replenish the earth. Man was, therefore, created to reflect God's ability to reproduce. God is a God of reproduction. He reproduced Himself in man and woman, and gave them the ability and instruction to reproduce themselves. By doing so, they would replenish the earth with the image of God in them.

Unfortunately, Man sinned against God and tarnished His image in them. The judgement God pronounced shows the extent to which God's image in them was damaged[3]. From then on, they would no longer reproduce after the image of God, but rather, after their own tarnished and damaged image. The bible says that Adam begot *a son* in his own likeness, after his image, and named him Seth.[4] Centuries later David confessed, *"Behold, I was brought forth in iniquity, and in sin my mother conceived me".*[5]

However, thank God for Jesus, Whose death and resurrection has redeemed humanity and is restoring men and women to their original glory and image of God. Through Jesus Christ both man and woman can now fulfil their God-ordained purpose on earth.

Designed to Create Life

Woman, created in God's image was designed to reproduce and carry life. God set a pattern within the blueprint of woman for this function. This pattern reflects the aspect of God's nature as life-giver. God is the giver of life. His Spirit is the One Who brooded over the surface of a dark, void and chaotic world, and then the Word came and creation was birthed. All of creation came forth from God's womb.

Job 38:8

"...Who shut in the sea with door when it burst forth and issued from the womb?"

Woman reflects God's nature as life-giver. Before God created woman, man carried the seed of humanity in his loins. However, there was no one with the capacity to reproduce that seed. God's word says that so long as the earth remains there will be seedtime and harvest.[6] Yet, man's seed would have remained dormant and unfruitful, if God had not created woman. For Man to be fruitful and multiply God created woman with the ability and capability to receive the seed of man, multiply, incubate, nurture, labour, birth and nourish it.

Woman was designed to receive, reproduce and multiply, nurture and give life! God designed and gave her the capacity to perform this function. I believe the most awesome and wonderful thing on earth is when a woman takes seed. It is almost as if she becomes instantly connected with God and joins hands with Him to create a new soul. It seems like heaven erupts with shouts of *'Hallelujah'*, as the woman links wombs with God to birth life, fulfilling God's purpose of filling the earth with people. Woman, mother of all living, possesses one of the most awesome attributes of God!

However, her God-given capacity to multiply seed and birth life goes beyond the physical. Whatever a woman receives she multiplies, because she was created to multiply seed. For example, if a woman receives love, she multiplies it and gives back more than love. I am certain the woman in Proverbs 31 had a very loving spouse, because she could never have achieved all she did without the love of a faithful husband.

If a woman receives insults and abuse, she multiplies just that. Why do you think a woman never forgets a fight she had with her husband five years ago? She remembers every word that was said because it lies within her, incubating and multiplying. She nurtures the words said during the fight and they grow and grow. One day, the man returns from work, and she is gone, never to return again, because 'the baby is out'! As William Congreve said, hell has no fury like a woman scorned.[6]

Woman, you are fearfully and wonderfully made. Go on, take a good look at yourself in the mirror and declare to yourself *"I am fearfully and wonderfully made in the image of God. I am designed for purpose!"*

REFLECTION QUESTIONS

1. Think about the way your culture defines women. What are some of the things you have learnt about your own body from your particular culture? Are they positive or negative?
2. Stand in front of a mirror (preferably naked) and take a good look at yourself. What do you see? Write down what you see.
3. Knowing that the scriptures say that we were created in God's image, how does what you see in the mirror reflect God's image in you?
4. Now, declare over and over again to yourself, *"I am fearfully and wonderfully made. I am designed for purpose!"*

Notes
1. Philippians 2:5-11
2. Isaiah 9:6
3. Psalm 51:5
4. Genesis 3
5. Genesis 5:3
6. Genesis 8:22
7. William Congreve, in *The mourning bride*, 1697

Chapter Five

A Unique System

"God's design for the woman as life-giver goes beyond her physical abilities. It permeates her entire makeup as a female... She is meant to conceive, develop, and give new life to, or "incubate" what she receives into herself." – Dr. Myles Monroe

Lessons from 'Mother Earth'

We have established so far that the purpose of a thing determines design. Woman has been created uniquely and intricately in every sense of her being. God designed her to accomplish the dynamic and important task of taking seed, incubating, multiplying and birthing it. Woman has been created and designed to reproduce the human race.

Reproduction is the process by which organisms produce more organisms like themselves. All living things, including humans, reproduce. This is one of the things that set us apart from non-living matter. The reproductive system is essential to keeping the species alive. The day we stop reproducing is the day the human race will begin the journey to extinction.

All life starts with a seed, which must be incubated, nurtured and nourished for it to grow and bear fruit. Every plant seed needs soil (earth) to incubate and germinate. Without soil, the seed will not germinate. Even seeds germinated in cotton wool are eventually transplanted into soil so they can flourish. Jesus said, *"I tell you the truth, unless a kernel of wheat falls to the ground and dies, it remains only a single seed. But if it dies, it produces many seeds."*[1] Every seed had to be incubated in soil, earth or ground to germinate before it can multiply, otherwise it remains alone and unfruitful. The seed multiplies, grows and bears fruit. Within the fruit are more seeds which, when planted again, reproduce and bear more fruit. This is the cycle of life.

In this capacity, the human race is no different from animals or plants. The male seed needs the soil of the woman's womb to incubate and grow. When the seed is planted in the woman's womb, it is nurtured and grows. The fruit of that seed is the human baby who is born, and who grows up to continue the cycle. However, woman's role within that process and cycle is very crucial and essential because without her body and womb, the seed remains alone and unfruitful. Even foetuses which start life in a test tube are eventually transplanted into a real womb. Hence, without woman's womb and body, the seed of man will become extinct. Without the female reproductive system, there would be no perpetuation of life.

Although the female is dependent on the male seed to fertilize her egg, she is the sole person who carries the offspring through pregnancy and childbirth. Through this reproductive process, children are born, and families are continued. If people didn't reproduce, families would die out and the human race would cease to exist. The command to multiply and replenish the earth would never be fulfilled without the woman. This is how essential woman is to the purposes of God.

Let's now take a closer look at the female anatomy to discover the wonder and awesome features God placed in woman.[2]

An Intricate Design

For woman to fulfil her function to reproduce and nurture life, God created her with a unique reproductive system. Unlike its male counterpart, the female reproductive system is almost entirely hidden within the pelvis. I believe this is an indication of the hidden strengths of woman.

I am not a biologist so I will not give an in-depth description of the female reproductive system. However, I will give a brief overview of what it consists of. To enable her to reproduce, God has given woman the following attributes, which are exclusive to her.

Brain-wiring

Men and women have differences that transcend the physical. It is no secret that men and women think and act differently. Any married couple will tell you stories about the various gender-based antics of their spouses, and numerous jokes and stories have been written about the differences between men and women. Many of these jokes attempt to determine which brain is better, the male or the female. Some of these jokes are quite hilarious.

A husband read an article to his wife about how many words women use a day.... 30,000 to a man's 15,000.

"The reason has to be because we have to repeat everything to men...," the wife replied,

The husband then turned to his wife and asked, *"What?"*

Men and women's brains are wired differently. God in his infinite wisdom has designed and wired the female brain to function according to purpose. The brain wiring of the female is what controls her reproductive system.

The hypothalamus, which is a tiny structure located at the base of the brain is smaller in size in women. However, the hypothalamus has been designed by God to send messages to the pituitary gland at the onset of puberty. The pituitary gland is also located at the base of the brain and produces the hormones that trigger the reproductive cycle. Hence, puberty in females, therefore, starts with changes in the hypothalamus that causes the pituitary gland to release the hormones or chemicals that are necessary for reproduction.

1. Internal Reproductive Organs

As said earlier, most of the female reproductive organs are hidden within the pelvis. God designed woman to possess the following:

Ovaries

These are two oval-shaped organs that produce, store, and release eggs for fertilization. The process of releasing eggs into the fallopian tubes is called ovulation. Each ovary measures about 4cm to 5cm in a grown woman. When a baby girl is born, her ovaries contain hundreds of thousands of eggs, which remain inactive until puberty begins. I believe that right from birth, God placed in every woman all that is needed to reproduce and give life.

A mature egg is released from the ovaries during each normal menstrual cycle. Each time an egg is released the body must be prepared to nourish a fertilized and developing embryo. The ovaries also produce some of the female sex hormones.

Fallopian Tubes

These are two tubes, each attached to a side of the uterus (womb). The fallopian tubes are about 10 cm long and about as wide as a piece of spaghetti. The tubes are designed to transport the eggs from the ovaries into the uterus. When an egg leaves the ovary, it enters the fallopian tube and is pushed down the narrow passageway toward the uterus. Fertilization usually occurs in the fallopian tube and then the fertilized egg travels down into the uterus to be 'planted'

Uterus

The uterus or womb is a small muscular organ roughly the size and shape of an upside-down pear. The uterus contains some of the strongest muscles in the female body. These muscles are able to expand and contract to accommodate a growing foetus and then help push the baby out during labour. It has an inner cavity lining, called the endometrium, which is rich in blood vessels. This lining builds up, matures, and sheds over the course of a woman's monthly menstrual cycle. The biological purpose of the lining is to serve as rich 'soil' for a fertilized egg to plant itself in. The fertilized egg travels from the fallopian tubes to the uterus and implants itself in the uterine lining.

Vagina

This is a hollow tube that extends from the vaginal opening to the uterus and has muscular walls that can expand and contract. This ability to expand and contract allows the vagina to accommodate something as big and wide as a baby. The vagina is for sexual intercourse to receive the male seed (sperm). It also provides the route for menstrual blood to leave the uterus and acts as the 'birth canal', the channel through which the baby is delivered.

2. Hormones

These are chemical messengers that carry signals from one cell (or group of cells) to another via the blood. A woman's body produces several hormones to aid the process of reproduction; below is a list of three of the predominant ones.

- **Oestrogen**: This influences the reconstruction of the endometrium, the inner cavity lining of the uterus.
- **Progesterone**: This is essential for the development of an embryo. It maintains the thickness of the endometrial wall, so that the fertilized egg can be implanted. High levels of progesterone and oestrogen cause milk glands to grow and prepare for breast-feeding.
- **Oxytocin**: This is produced in the pituitary gland and triggers the contractions at the end of pregnancy to cause

the baby to be delivered. It also causes the milk ducts to contract during lactation (breast-feeding).

3. Breasts

Breasts are external organs that God designed and created for nurturing a new born baby. Despite its role as an object of human sexuality, the biological purpose of the breast is to nourish one's child. The breasts contain mammary glands that secrete milk after childbirth. Human breasts come in all shapes and sizes but perform the same task of nourishing and nurturing. This is the beauty of God's creation in woman.

Functioning Like Clockwork

One of the most interesting things about the female body is the way it functions, almost like clockwork or an orchestra, pre-rehearsed and tuned-up. As said earlier, the female baby is born with thousands of eggs in her ovaries. She obviously comes prepared to fulfil her function, since her male counterpart only develops sperm at puberty.

Many cultures 'celebrate' puberty by performing various rites. Unfortunately, some of these rites cast a shadow and leave a negative impression on the minds of the participants. Years ago, a woman told me that as part of her puberty rites, she was given a boiled egg to swallow whole! Now, I don't know the significance of that, but I am sure it was not a pleasant experience for her! However, other cultures 'celebrate' puberty with much fanfare.

Regardless of how a particular culture acknowledges it, puberty is a very important time in a woman's life. It is an amazing thing to watch a girl grow up from childhood to puberty! Almost overnight, she begins to develop and her body begins to change. I have watched my own daughter, Nobelle, grow up and I am seeing the same pattern in my nieces and friends' daughters. With Nobelle, first came the trainer bras, oh my goodness, and then me teasing her about growing up. After that came her menstrual period! Fortunately we had already discussed these things so she was well informed. However, I watched with awe as her body began to change, almost on cue! Her hips began to broaden and her breast began to develop. I also noticed that she was becoming more aware of her body. Unfortunately for me, she also began to notice boys noticing her. I once caught a young man eyeing her. He felt very embarrassed when he realised I was watching him watch her and quickly turned his eyes!

Almost overnight, my baby has grown up into a beautiful young woman, without anyone asking or telling her to. Her body has just developed, as God had planned it; no one could do to hinder or alter that!

This is the beauty of the woman's body, fearfully and wonderfully made in God's image, with every organ in its rightful place and communicating with one another, as scheduled by God. Despite the fact that women come in all shapes, sizes, heights and weights, as if one cue from a divine source, the female body begins to transform, growing and developing to fulfil God-given function and purpose. Indeed, the human female body is a unique and mean 'machine' created by God!

We will further discuss the way the female reproductive system works in the next chapter. Meanwhile, take a few minutes to pause and think about over your own body. In the light of what you've just read, think of how you grew up. Consider the changes your body went through and the awkwardness you felt, not quite knowing why your body was developing so fast and why your emotions and moods were all over the place

Nobelle came home from college yesterday and said, *"Mummy I need to speak to you about stuff."* I told her we would have a chat later. However, because of the urgency to finish this book, I totally forgot to ask her what the matter was, until this afternoon Cobby said to me, you need to speak to Nobelle because she is upset about something. I noticed she had been crying and asked her what was wrong. She said she was struggling with her workload and everything seemed to be on top her. I looked at her, smiled and said, *"Perhaps you are ovulating."* She said yes, we had a chat and a cuddle and she was okay again. I thought to myself, praise God, she is going through this, because it just shows that she is a woman through and through, and this is why I am dedicating this book to her.

As you ponder over these things, thank God He created you a WOMAN!

REFLECTION QUESTIONS

1. Review what you have just read. Are you beginning to see the intricate details and features God deliberately put in woman?

2. Cast your mind back to your years of puberty. Do you remember what it felt like? Can you describe some of the changes that took place?

3. Again, think of how your culture views and celebrates puberty. Is it a positive or negative experience, and how has that influenced your life?

4. What must change in the way you think about yourself? Write it down and begin to pray about it.

Notes

1. John 12:24
2. The information in this Chapter has been gathered through several years of studying and reading various books and articles about woman's anatomy and physiology, including:
3. Nemours Foundation, Kid's Health for Parents, "Female Reproductive System", http://www.kidshealth.org/parent/general/body_basics/ female_reproductive_system.html

Chapter Six

THE LIFE-GIVING PROCESS

The Ultimate Creative Activity

The words "you are pregnant" can bring all sorts of emotions to a woman, depending on whether the pregnancy was planned or unplanned, wanted or unwanted. For the unplanned and unwanted, those three words could be the most devastating and life-shattering words they would hear in a long while. For the planned and wanted, it would be the most delightful and joyous piece of news ever received. Whether planned or unplanned, the birth of a child is one of the most beautiful events one could ever anticipate or celebrate. Pregnancy is the ultimate creative activity.

My friend 'Rose' (not her real name) is pregnant and I am so excited about it. Especially, because it took her such a long time to conceive! I am just looking forward to the day I'll receive the call saying 'Rose' has delivered her baby. I will shout 'Hallelujah' because God has done it again! He has created life through the womb of yet another woman.

1. Ovulation[1]

The life-giving process starts way before a woman interacts with a man. It begins with ovulation. As said in the previous chapter, at puberty, the hypothalamus sends messages to the pituitary gland, which begins to releases the hormones that trigger ovulation. During ovulation, an egg is released from one of the ovaries, ready for fertilization and implanting in the uterus. The egg travels into the uterus (womb) down the fallopian tube.

Menstruation

Many cultural and religious practices portray menstruation as dirty or filthy. Some religions even believe a woman cannot approach God whilst she is menstruating because she is ritually unclean. A coupe of days ago someone asked me if it was acceptable to fast during her period. She had recently become a Christian and her previous religion deemed it inappropriate for a woman to fast during menstruation because she was dirty. I also read a 'joke' about God being displeased with a woman because she had washed in the river during her period, thus, ruining the taste of fish forever! Menstruation is part of woman's God-given process of life-creation and there is nothing unclean or filthy about it. It is messy but does not make you unclean.

During ovulation, the ovaries release an egg, which moves towards the uterus, ready for fertilization and with an expectation that it would meet a sperm, and be implanted in the uterus. Immediately, the endometrial walls begin to thicken with blood, preparing for implantation. When the egg is not fertilized and planted, the uterus sheds its lining, the *endometrium*, which results in the flow of the menstrual blood. This is what we call menstruation or a period.

This is actually one of the wonders of creation, that from a very young age when puberty commences, month after month, sometimes for over forty years, the female body goes through the same experience, the ovaries releasing an egg every month, each time with the expectation that it would be fertilized. Every month, year after year, God gives women an opportunity to create and birth life. What an awesome reality!

2. Pregnancy

Fertilization takes place when the woman receives and takes a sperm from a man. Pregnancy occurs when the egg becomes fertilized and is implanted in the uterus. The fertilized egg instantly begins to multiply. Remember, God designed woman's body to multiply every thing everything she receives. The cells in the fertilized egg multiply very rapidly and begin to develop into a foetus. The male sperm is invisible to the human eye and tinier that the tip of a needle. Yet, when it encounters the female egg, it begins to multiply and grow.

It is amazing that the world is full of billions of people and every single one of them came into being because a woman took the tiny seed of a man, incubated, multiplied and birthed it! There is no other way a human being can be created outside of this process. Even in creating test tube babies, doctors still have to join together a sperm and an egg, and as mentioned earlier, transplant the fertilized egg back into a womb.

Pregnancy lasts for nine months from fertilization to birth. During this period development continues as cells multiply, move, and differentiate. The foetus is nurtured and incubated within the womb until labour, whilst the woman's body goes through complete transformation. Below is a list (not necessarily in order of occurrence) of some of the changes that occur in a woman's body during pregnancy:

1. Menstruation ceases as the lining of the womb is no longer shed. The lining thickens to create a perfect environment of warmth and protection for the foetus.

2. The hormonal levels in her body change as the woman's body increases production in order to prevent miscarriage. These hormones can wreck havoc with her body, as her brain chemistry also alters.

3. Placenta, a disk-like structure that adheres to the inner lining of the womb is formed and is connected to the umbilical cord. Oxygen and nourishment come from the mother's blood via the placenta.

4. One of the greatest unsolved mysteries in immunology is how the placenta survives for nine months without being rejected by the mother's immune system, since every cell of the placenta carries the father's genes. Thus the placenta is as foreign to the mother as a kidney transplant would be, yet it thrives. Despite years of research, the reason for this privileged status remains unknown.

5. The nutrients in the woman's blood are directed firstly to the foetus and secondly to her. The interesting thing is that the woman has no control of this, as her body works, almost like a machine to preserve the life of the

foetus. Whether she eats or not, the foetus draws nutrients from the pregnant woman's blood. A woman, therefore, endangers her own life, as well as that the foetus, if she does not eat properly. There are also limitations on what she can eat.

6. Blood is carried from the foetus to the placenta and from the placenta to the foetus via veins and arteries in the umbilical cord. The foetus continues to grow in the womb, hidden from human eye, and only seen on the outside as a bulge on the woman's body.

7. Amniotic fluid, which is also called 'water' and membrane in the womb cushion and protect the foetus against bumps and jolts to the mother's body.

8. The centre of gravity of the mother changes so that she can keep her balance. In reality because of the size of the bulge, a pregnant woman should tilt over. However, her body adjusts itself by changing her centre of gravity. If you have ever seen an African pregnant woman returning home from the farm, you will know what I mean. She is heavily pregnant, yet, has one child secured on her back, a basket of foodstuff balanced on her head and is holding another child by the hand!

9. The woman's breasts begin to alter and enlarge, preparing for lactation.

Pregnancy is a very exciting time, despite the challenges and worries. There is so much expectation as the mother begins to prepare for her soon-to-be-born child, buying clothes, preparing a cot or crib, etc.

During pregnancy, the mother's entire body shifts focus to the task of developing and preserving the new life within her. God is the Giver of life and He created woman to link up with heaven to create life. Every part of woman's body has been pre-conditioned by God to perform this dynamic feat. Woman you are more important to God and humanity than you have ever acknowledged. Go on, clap for yourself! Celebrate yourself! Give glory to God for His awesome and wonderful creation!

Before we proceed and discuss the ability of a mother to labour and deliver her baby, I would like to take a moment to talk briefly about some other aspects of taking seed, namely barrenness, miscarriage, stillbirth, abortion and menopause.

Barrenness
Since we have been designed to take seed and birth life, barrenness is very painful, as it goes against the very nature of woman. Many women have been ridiculed and accused of not being woman enough because they are unfruitful. The shame that many women face because of this is unimaginable. Many spend huge amounts of money, sometimes even borrowing, to seek medical help to conceive

Rachel expressed it eloquently when she cried to Jacob, *"Give me children or I else die!"*[2] Her barrenness was working against her nature as a woman and the very essence of her being. Sarah, Hannah and Elizabeth all despaired because they were considered barren.

I know several women who have not had a child yet, but we are praying and trusting God to 'open their wombs'. He is merciful and He will answer. Even now, I pray for every barren or infertile married woman reading this book. I pray in the name of Jesus Christ, that God will open up your womb and cause you to conceive. I pray that you will take seed, which shall multiply and grow in you; you shall carry it till term and birth a healthy baby. You will never miscarry again; you will carry till full term. I pray that God will grant you favour because children are a reward from Him. May God cause you to deliver all your children,[3] in Jesus' Name! Amen. Please remember to write or send us your testimonies. Amen.

However, many other women who have been declared barren have taken the opportunity and adopted and nurture children who are not theirs by birth. *The nurturing instinct in woman is limitless and can be activated at any time.*

Miscarriage and Stillbirth

Miscarriage is a very painful thing for any woman. Miscarriage also goes against the very nature and grain of the feminine nature. Stillbirth is also one of the greatest misfortunes that could ever befall a woman. It is something one wouldn't wish on their worst enemy. Isaiah 26:17-18 describes the pain of stillbirth,

"As a woman with child drawing near the time of her delivery is in pain and writhes and cries out in her pangs,

so we have been before You (at Your presence), O Lord. We have been with child, we have been writhing and in pain; we have, as it were, brought forth [only] wind. We have not wrought any deliverance in the earth, and the inhabitants of the world [of Israel] have not yet been born".

Abortion

Abortion has become a major issue of concern in our modern world, especially because it has become rampant among teenage girls. Abortion takes place when a woman takes seed but, for whatever reason, decides she does not want the pregnancy, and so deliberately has it terminated.

If miscarriage and stillbirth go against the nature of woman, then abortion violates the very essence of her being! Women have to be very careful when making the decision to terminate a pregnancy. In the bible, Onan, the son of Judah, spilled his semen on the ground anytime he went into Tamar, his late brother's wife because he was reluctant to produce children with her. His actions displeased God and so He killed him.[4] If God considered the spillage or wastage of seed a sin against Him, how much more the rejection and termination of potential life from seed already taken?

Abortion must never be an option, should a woman become pregnant in unfortunate circumstances. However, if you have had an abortion before, please know that Jesus Christ loves you and is ready to forgive you. All you need to do is to repent and ask for forgiveness.

Menopause

Menopause is when a woman's monthly periods cease, signifying the end of her childbearing years. The ovaries stop releasing eggs as the hormonal levels decrease. Menopause is often viewed as a negative thing because of the various problems that accompany it. It is interesting to note that the age of menopause is decreasing among women, and some women commence as early as their late thirties.

The post-menopausal years of a woman do not necessarily have to be negative as strengths, skills and abilities could be channelled elsewhere.

3. Labour

This is a very crucial and stressful, yet, awesome and rewarding stage of the life-creating process. The mother is often tired and has not much control over her body. She waits in anticipation and anxiety for the process of labour to begin.

The period of labour is one of much pain and effort. The severity of the pain and effort is due to the size of the baby. What is incredible about labour is that the foetus the mother is birthing is larger than the birth canal, the vagina. It is just remarkable how God designed and built the female body to perform this God-given function.

It is said that the pressure exerted on a woman's body during delivery would kill a man! The pressure is so great that a man's body could not physically hold it. The magnitude of God's grace to a woman during labour is immeasurable. Personally, I believe delivering a baby is both a physical and spiritual experience, because as she approaches delivery, the mother' body alters almost supernaturally, enabling her to accomplish what is almost impossible under any other circumstance.

The pelvis begins to shift, open up and re-align itself for labour and delivery. The foetus turns and aligns itself upside down, with its head toward the cervix. The walls of the womb begin to contract (stimulated by the hormone oxytocin), which is an indication that it is time for the baby to be delivered.

The contractions cause the cervix to begin to widen and open, and the baby's head presses on the cervix, which begins to relax and further widen in readiness for the baby to come out. When the cervix is fully dilated, with every nerve, muscle, fibre, energy and willpower, the mother pushes the life in her out through the vagina, which has enlarged to become the birth canal. There is a sense of great expectation, excitement and joy as a new life is given to the world again!

This is the miracle of life, that a 7-pound (or more) baby can be pushed through a 10cm hole! This is the miracle of life that woman's body can sustain the pressure and pain. Indeed, God has fearfully and wonderfully created us. Hallelujah!

The umbilical cord is cut, signifying the separation of the new life birthed with that of the mother's womb. The final stage of the birth process involves the delivery of the placenta. It separates itself from the lining of the womb, and through further contractions of the womb, the woman's body expels it. The minute the placenta is shed, one life-birthing cycle ends and the body begins to prepare itself, in readiness to commence another. The ovaries begin to release eggs again in anticipation of fertilization.

The impact of this awesome experience on me is huge, as it gives me more revelation about our awe-inspiring God. The power and wonder of our invisible God is truly manifested in this stupendous achievement through women. Woman, you deserve a standing ovation! God has truly honoured and empowered you. Hallelujah!

4. Lactation and Nursing

The delivery of a baby, or new life, is not the conclusion of the life-giving process. Once the baby's out the woman feeds it at her breast. Lactation, the act of producing and releasing breast milk, is a complicated process that begins during pregnancy. Increased levels of hormones cause the milk glands in the breasts to grow and get ready for making milk. After birth, the milk glands begin to produce milk.

When the newborn baby then sucks the nipple, a nerve impulse travels from the breast to the brain and causes another chemical, oxytocin, to be released. This then causes the milk glands and milk ducts to contract and milk is released into the sucking baby's mouth.

The milk produced by the breast is one of a kind, and all attempts by pharmaceutical companies to duplicate it have been only partially successful. Breast milk contains the exact proportions of fats, proteins, carbohydrates, vitamins, minerals, and water that the newborn child requires. It also contains thousands of different antibodies to protect the baby from potential infections, which manufactured formula lacks. Breastfeeding creates and allow a special bond and closeness between mother and infant and is highly recommended.

The mother continues to nourish and nurture the life that has been created through her. In this the mother truly reflects the nature of God as El-Shaddai – the many breasted One.[5] The baby continues to draw from the mother and its life and survival is solely dependent on her. The picture of a lactating mother is a very intimate and alluring one.

The reproductive capacity of woman influences every area of her life. Dr James Dobson said that this reproductive ability results in a greater appreciation for stability, security and enduring human relationships in women. A mother never ceases to be a mother till death. The bible is right in asking, can a woman forget her nursing child and not have compassion on the son of her womb?[6] As another person rightly said, a woman can never forget her children because they won't let her!

Revelation Has Come, Arise and Shine

Writing this chapter has left me feeling very overwhelmed. I travel the nations with a mandate from God to stir up His daughters, and raise, restore and release them to work. Many of the women I encounter are broken, wounded, afraid, helpless and weak. Many have no real sense or experience of God's love for them, or of the value He places on their lives, even though they are His children. Many of the women lack purpose and vision and have no real perspective of a fruitful life in God's kingdom. I am not only referring to women in Africa, but also, women in the Western world. Whenever I think of these women my heart aches.

However, God has given me good news for all women. God wants to put value on you once again. Through Jesus Christ, God is restoring you once again. The previous chapter and this one have revealed deep truths about you, woman. Yes, you! You are fearfully and wonderfully made in God's image. His nature is within you. His strength and power are yours to possess. His favour is upon you. Arise and shine WOMAN, for God's light has come and His glory has risen upon you.[7] ARISE, WOMAN! SHINE!

REFLECTION QUESTIONS

1. Review and ponder over the Life-Giving Process. How does that reflect the image of God in women?
2. What are the essential lessons this chapter has taught you? Write them down and prayerfully ponder over them.
3. What must change in your thinking and life?
4. Are you struggling with some of the issues raised – barrenness, miscarriage, abortion or menopause? Please pray and continue to trust in the Lord, knowing that He loves and cares for you.

Notes

1. The information in this Chapter has been gathered through several years of studying and reading various books and articles about woman's anatomy and physiology, including: Nemours Foundation, Kid's Health for Parents, "Female Reproductive System", http://www.kidshealth.org/parent/general/body_basics/female_reproductive_system.htm
2. Genesis 30:1
3. Isaiah 49:25

4. Genesis 38:6-10
5. El-Shaddai is on of the Hebrew names of God and is the name by which God was known to Abraham, Isaac, and Jacob - Ex. 6:2, 3. El-Shaddai can be translated as "He who is sufficient", "The many breasted one" or "He who satisfies"
6. Isaiah 49:15
7. Isaiah 60:1

Chapter Seven

SPIRITUAL LESSONS FROM A PHYSICAL REALITY

"But the basic reality of God is plain enough. Open your eyes and there it is! By taking a long and thoughtful look at what God has created, people have always been able to see what their eyes as such can't see: eternal power, for instance, and the mystery of His divine being. So nobody has a good excuse." Romans 1:19-20 (TM)

The Emperor's New Clothes

Most people are familiar with the tale of the emperor's new clothes, which is about an emperor who lived many years ago, and who was very fond of his clothes. One day, two swindlers visited him and said they could make the finest suit of clothes from the most beautiful cloth. This cloth, however, also had a special quality that made it invisible to anyone who was stupid. With much eagerness, the emperor gave the two men a huge sum of money to make the fabric and clothes.

Being a bit nervous about whether he himself would be able to see the cloth, the emperor sent two of his trusted men to view it. Neither of them wanted to appear stupid by admitting that they could not see the cloth, and so they praised it. All the townspeople had also heard of the cloth and were anxious not to appear stupid.

67

The day came for the emperor to try on his new clothes. He allowed himself to be dressed in his new clothes that were invisible to the stupid. Unwilling to admit that he was too stupid to see what he was wearing, the emperor ordered a grand parade and rode through town, all dressed up in his special clothes.

Of course, all the townspeople wildly praised the magnificent clothes of the emperor, afraid to admit that they could not see them, until a small child said, *"But he has nothing on!"* This was whispered from person to person until everyone in the crowd was shouting that the emperor had nothing on. The emperor heard it and felt that they were correct, but held his head high and finished the procession.[1]

Physical Precedes Spiritual

You may ask, *"What is the moral of this story and how relevant is it to this chapter?"* Well, it is this: you can never try and make something out of nothing. Only God could make something out of nothing. Since then, everything we see, smell or touch originates from something that already exists. The bible says there is nothing new under the sun.[2]

The Word of God teaches us that the visible reveals the invisible[3], unlike the emperor's new clothes, which tried to use the invisible to display the visible. The scripture also tells us that the physical precedes the spiritual.

1 Corinthians 15:46-49

"The spiritual did not come first, but the natural, and after that the spiritual. The first man was of the dust of the earth,

the second man from heaven. As was the earthly man, so are those who are of the earth; and as is the man from heaven, so also are those who are of heaven. And just as we have borne the likeness of the earthly man, so shall we bear the likeness of the man from heaven."

The holy nation of Israel was first physical[4], and then following the death, resurrection and ascension of Jesus Christ, became spiritual[5]. Moses' tabernacle was also a representation of the heavenly one.[6] The book of Colossians describes Jesus as the image of the invisible God,[7] and Jesus Himself said that if you have seen Him you have seen the Father.[8] Therefore, we can learn essential spiritual lessons by studying or observing the physical. Woman was fearfully and wonderfully made in the image of God, and so by studying her physique, we are bound to discover hidden spiritual parallels and truths. In other words, the female body possesses a physical form of glory, which could be demonstrated spiritually, through the empowerment of the Holy Spirit.

Seven Important Lessons

Complete and Full in Christ

It is without doubt that woman was created in God's image; therefore, her physical body reflects aspects of the divine nature – strengths, abilities and characteristics. Even though sin marred the nature of humanity, through Jesus Christ we are restored again. The fullness of God dwells in Christ and we are complete in Him.[9]

We have been made whole in Christ, and therefore, we can attain and achieve all that God has purposed for us. We have been made whole in Christ and can exhibit those spiritual qualities that display the image of God in us.

Designed to Receive

God designed woman to receive. A woman's perception and intuition help her to receive. She is quick to perceive and within her spirit she can catch and sense things that are not very obvious to others. It does not matter what it is, so long as a woman receives it, it becomes seed. In the physical she is uniquely designed to receive a sperm (male seed), and this also reflects her nature in the spirit. A woman will receive and take anything – sperm, love or hatred, a business idea, a prayer need, a burden for a sick friend, a news bulletin or a prayer request. Instantly, what she receives becomes a seed in her, with a full potential to germinate and bear fruit.

All a woman needs is a seed. It is unfortunate that these days, women can conceive and have children without intimacy with a man, just by acquiring a test tube of sperm. However, this proves the point that woman was designed as such. Mary, the mother of Jesus received a word from the Angel Gabriel that she would conceive and bear a child, and she instantly received the word and took the seed of the Holy Spirit.

This is something husbands must remember, that a woman was designed to receive and whatever she receives becomes seed in her being. Perhaps, that is why the scripture instructs men to love their wives. When a woman receives love, it becomes a seed of love in her, which she multiplies and brings forth fruits of love. What we receive in the natural is a mere shadow of what we can receive in the spirit as women.

Another amazing aspect of woman is that she is not limited to one seed. She has the ability to take more than one seed at a time, incubate them in her womb and birth them. Women who carry multiple births demonstrate this ability. Hence, a woman can take on more than one project, idea or prayer request.

Multiplies What She Receives

As she is in the natural, so is she in the spirit, therefore, whatever a woman receives she multiplies. A woman receives a male seed and instantly her body begins to multiply and nurture it. Just as the seed multiples, incubates and grows, a woman will multiply, incubate and cause whatever she receives to grow.

If a wife received love from her husband, she would multiply that love, nurture and cause it to grow. She would grow to love, cherish and adore him more and more. She would honour and respect him, and protect him with her very life, if necessary. Interestingly, because of the way God created men, the wife's expressions of love, would cause her husband to shower more love on her, which she would further receive and multiply. This cycle of love is the foundation of a good marriage.

However, if a woman is given abuse or insults, she is going to receive, multiply and incubate just that, and who knows what she would bring forth! This reminds me of a story I heard a while ago:

A man and his wife were having some problems at home and were giving each other the silent treatment. After about a week, the man suddenly realized that the next day, he would need his wife to wake him at 5:00am for an early morning business flight. Not wanting to be the first to break the silence, he wrote on a piece of paper, *"Please wake me at 5:00am,"* and left it where he knew she would find it.

The next morning, the man woke up, only to discover it was 9:00am and he had missed his flight. Furious, he was about to go and ask his wife why she hadn't woken him up, when he noticed a piece of paper by the bed. The paper said, *"It is 5:00am. Wake up."*

Only a woman could come up with something like that! Women always multiply what they receive. Like a snowball effect, whatever you give to a woman will multiply in her hands. Give her a vision, a business idea or a burden for a sick friend, a city or nation. Once she receives it as seed, she will take it into her spiritual womb, incubate and multiply it.

We must, therefore, be careful what seeds we take, as women. Knowing our ability to multiply and reproduce, we must choose our seeds very carefully. We will discuss this in more detail in Chapter 9.

Births What She Has Multiplied

Whatever a woman receives she multiplies, and whatever she multiplies, she births. It is a known fact that more women attend prayer meetings and that there are more women intercessors than men.

A woman can take an idea or a prayer topic to heart and will pray and work through it till it manifests. Bishop George Searight, an American preacher said, *"When I have a seed, an idea or problem, I give it to my wife. She goes down on her knee and labours until she births the answer."*

Dr. Myles Monroe also said, *"Just as a womb nourishes a foetus during development and an incubator protects premature or sick babies, a woman has a nurturing instinct that can be a powerful source of help and encouragement to others. If a man wants something prayed about, he should tell a woman. She will take the circumstance into her spiritual womb, where she meets with God in her inner being, incubate it for months if necessary, and bring forth a solution. She won't give up until she hears from God."*

A Pastor dreamt that he had died and gone to heaven, where God was giving out rewards. He realized that most of the people around him were his congregation members, which made him very glad. The Lord began to hand out crowns, calling each person by name. All the crowns were of different styles, shapes and sizes; and some had more gems and precious stones than others. Suddenly, God brought out the most beautiful crown the pastor had ever seen. This crown had very large precious stones, which sparkled in the light, reflecting the colours of the rainbow. The pastor thought, *"Surely, this must be my crown!"* After all, he had worked so hard and led many to the Lord, and most of his congregation were with him in heaven.

But no, God called out a quite old lady in his church and placed the crown on her head. The pastor was perplexed, and asked God why. God said to him, *"Without her you would have no ministry, because everything you have achieved is because of her prayers."* God continued, *"Every time you go up to preach, this woman goes into the cloakroom and prays for you."*

The pastor woke up and realised it was only a dream. Yet, he was still perplexed by what he had heard in the dream and decided to verify it. The next Sunday, just before he was about to preach, he paused, walked through the puzzled congregation, and went to the cloakroom. Sure enough, he found the little old lady in the dream on her knees praying for him! This dear old lady had taken her pastor and his ministry as seeds in her spiritual womb, and travailed and laboured for him on her knees for years! The fruits in his life and ministry had been birthed through her prayers!

The bible says that *"Deep calls to deep,"* and when a woman takes seed into both her physical and spiritual wombs, she becomes directly connected with the 'womb' of God. She is instantly linked with the ultimate Life-Giver and something profound takes place, as together, a new life is birthed.

The gospels give many examples of women who received and multiplied: the woman at the well, the gentile woman who wanted her daughter healed (she would even settle for crumbs as long as she received something from Jesus), and Mary, the mother of Jesus. Luke 8:1-3 mentions some more women in the bible

"Soon afterward, [Jesus] went on through towns and villages, preaching and bringing the good news (the Gospel) of the kingdom of God. And the Twelve [apostles] were with Him, and also some women who had been cured of evil spirits and diseases: Mary, called Magdalene, from whom seven demons had been   expelled; And Joanna, the wife of Chuza, Herod's household manager; and Susanna;

and many others, who ministered to and provided for Him and them out of their property and personal belongings."

Every one of these women had received a healing touch or deliverance from Jesus. They sacrifice all and followed Him, providing for Him from their substance. They were utterly devoted to Him and served Him with their all.

There are further lessons to be learnt from the ability of woman to labour and birth. The reason why a woman endures so much pain during childbirth is that what she is releasing from within her is much, much bigger that the channel through which she is releasing it! The determination with which she pushes and forces the baby out of her goes beyond the natural. This ability can be channelled into the areas of prayer, intercession, evangelism, and in fact, anything we set ourselves to do.

Perhaps, the vision or burden God has given you seems huge and impossible. Perhaps, the responsibility your pastor has placed on you appears too big. Praise God for that, because as you link up with the Holy Spirit, He will supply grace and enable you to do what God has put on your heart to do.

C. Peter Wagner thinks that certain spiritual gifts are gender biased, including intercession. He has interviewed several intercessors who have suggested that a woman's biological function of conception, gestation and the travail of giving birth might have something to do with it. Peter Wagner continued to say, *"A major ministry of intercession is to bring into being the purposes of God, and many describe some of their most intense periods of intercession as travail. Mothers know even better than could apostle Paul the full meaning of his statement, "My*

75

little children, for whom I labour in birth again until Christ is formed in you" (Gal. 4:19)."[10]

Strength to Endure

Pregnancy takes approximately nine months. It is an extended period of waiting and enduring patiently. The ability to wait and endure, knowing there is not much one can do until it is time for the baby to come out is one of the strengths of woman. She endures the nausea and sickness, weight gain/loss, backache, mood swings, swollen ankles and clothes that don't fit.

Yet, she is focused and has her eye on the goal - a new born baby boy or girl. She know that *'though it tarries it shall surely come',* so she endures and perseveres and presses on towards her day of delivery.

This is an asset the Church requires, as we face a world full of evil and woe, warring for our marriages, families, communities, cities and nations. Sometimes it is a real struggle to make change, as the things that work against us almost seem unmoveable and unshakeable. But, as women we have the ability to press on, focused and undeterred until change comes.

Nurtures the Child She Bears

Woman's nurturing ability goes beyond the delivery of her child. A woman breast or bottle feeds her child until it's time to wean him. She continues to take care of that child, almost indefinitely. Hannah weaned Samuel and released him to the Lord in the care of Eli. Yet every year she made and took him new clothes.[11]

A mother would sacrifice all for the welfare of her child. A mother would go to the ends of the earth to defend or protect her child. This is a natural ability that portrays the very nature of God as our Provider, Defender and Protector.

There appears to be an urgent need for 'disciplers' in the kingdom. Newly converted souls must be 'discipled', raised and nurtured to maturity. When I got saved almost thirty years ago, someone was assigned to disciple me. I attended discipleship classes, prayer meetings, etc, where I was nurtured and taught the basics of the Christian faith. There were times when I felt like giving up, but the people around me supported and nurtured me, teaching me how to pray, fast, study and live the scriptures and share the gospel. I became grounded in the Lord as a result of this.

Unfortunately, there appears to be a shortage of people who will take time and effort to disciple others. There are many Christians who have not acquired a solid foundation and are struggling with sin, temptation and personal weaknesses because they were not properly nurtured and discipled as young Christians. This is where, I believe, we come in as women. We have the natural ability to raise children. We can channel that ability into nurturing, nourishing and raising spiritual children for God. I know most women lead busy lives, but, I believe if we cared enough, we would ask God for strength and grace to do it.

Multifaceted in Nature and Ability
Women are multifaceted in nature and ability. My son Richard came into the kitchen and asked what I was doing. I was cooking

the evening's dinner and two other dishes for the weekend. He seemed very surprised and asked, *"How are you able to cook three dishes at the same time?"* I laughed, because what he did not realise was that I was also loading both washing machine and dishwasher, and doing some work on my computer at the same time! That is what you call multifaceted, multitalented and multitasked! And that too is a gift from the Lord to women!

Women who give birth, especially to twins or triplets, manifest skills that surpass those of a company executive, juggling their duties – changing nappies, bathing, feeding, burping, putting to sleep, washing clothes, sterilizing bottles, and still having time to cook and clean! Wow! Naturally women are able to do many things at once, e.g. cook, clean, bathe a child and speak on the telephone at the same time. We can also reflect this in the spirit.

Recently someone asked me, how do you do it Jennifer? This is because I am a wife, mother and homemaker, run a ministry, mentor several women, write, travel often to speak… and still make prayer a priority in my life! I answered, God gives grace and strength! God has made me a multifaceted human being and as I tune-in and rely on Him I am indeed able to do all things.

We need to begin to ask God to show us how we can use these abilities and capabilities to benefit His kingdom. The church needs our gifts more than it has been acknowledged. Women can give life to anything that is dead. What is dead in your community? What needs life? What needs nurturing? What can we influence? Just name it and we'll take it and transform and breathe life into it.

REFLECTION QUESTIONS

1. Review the spiritual lessons listed in this chapter. Can you identify any more lessons to be learnt? Write them down.
2. How do you think you can put these lessons into practice?
3. Ponder over the multifaceted qualities and abilities of woman. In what ways do you display these and how can you use them in your service to God?
4. What must change in your life and thinking? Write them down and pray over them.

Notes

1. Anderson, Hans Christian, "The Emperor's New Clothes", Houghton Mifflin Children's Books, 2004
2. Ecclesiastes 1:10
3. Romans 1:20
4. Exodus 19:5-6
5. 1 Peter 2:9
6. Exodus 19:5-6
7. Colossians 1:15
8. John 14:8-11
9. Colossians 2:9
10. Wagner, C. Peter, "Prayer Shield", Regal Books, USA, pg. 50
11. 1 Samuel 2:19

Chapter Eight

AIDS TO SPIRITUAL CONCEPTION

"Stay joined to me, and I will stay joined to you. Just as a branch cannot produce fruit unless it stays joined to the vine, you cannot produce fruit unless you stay joined to me. I am the vine, and you are the branches. If you stay joined to me, and I stay joined to you, then you will produce lots of fruit. But you cannot do anything without me" John 15:4-5 (CEV)

Vital to Survival

Experts advise that when you are trying to get pregnant, folic acid should be on your health checklist. This is because folic acid is one of the few nutrients known to prevent birth defects, such as spina bifida. Women who take the recommended daily dosage of folic acid reduce their baby's risk of some types of birth defects by 50 percent. Women who don't get enough may increase their chance of miscarriage or stillbirths. In preparing for and during pregnancy, iron also is another necessary nutrient, a deficiency of which can cause fatigue and weakness.[1]

We have already determined that the physical always has a bearing on the spiritual. As we are in the natural, so are we in the spirit. Just as there are important and essential things that must be on our natural health checklist if we want to have a baby, there must be certain crucial items on our spiritual 'health checklist,' if we want to be fruitful.

I would like to briefly discuss some of these things, since they are vital to our survival. Just as folic acid can prevent spina bifida and reduce the risk of miscarriage and stillbirth, and iron can reduce fatigue, there are certain basic Christian activities that can help us become more fruitful.

Aids to Spiritual Conception

1. The Word of God
Knowing and studying the scriptures helps us grow and mature spiritually. We nourish and keep our physical bodies strong and healthy with food daily. Without food and its nutrients, our bodies grow weak and cannot function properly. In the same way, we need to nourish and feed ourselves with God's word in order to grow and mature spiritually.

Hebrews 5:12-14
"For though by this time you ought to be teachers, you need someone to teach you again the first principles of the oracles of God; and you have come to need milk and not solid food. For everyone who partakes only of milk is unskilled in the word of righteousness, for he is a babe. But solid food belongs to those who are of full age ...who by reason of use have their senses exercised to discern both good and evil."

When we feed on God's word daily, it helps us to grow and become mature and fruitful Christians. Studying the bible also helps us to know God's thoughts and plans for us. This encourages us to trust Him as we wait on Him. David said, *"Remember the word to Your servant, upon which You have caused me to hope. This is my comfort in my affliction, for Your word has given me life."*[2] Studying the scriptures also helps us to know God's will, so that we can pursue it.

2. Prayer

Prayer is very essential to our walk with God. Without prayer we can achieve very little as Christians. This is because it is impossible for us to bear much fruit if we are not prayerful. We become weak and ineffective when we do not pray. If the word of God is our spiritual food, then prayer is our spiritual oxygen! Without it we die!

Prayer is about spending time in God's company and presence, talking and listening to Him. It is a two-way communication or interaction between God and His children. Communication is essential to the success of any relationship, and so prayer is the channel of communication between us and God. As fresh and constant communication is vital to any relationship, so is prayer essential to our relationship with God.

God wants us to talk to Him, chat with Him, discuss issues with Him, ask Him for things, ask questions and listen to His answers, confide in and get to know Him as father and friend. We spend time with God in prayer in order to express love, admiration or thanks or in order to receive from Him. Oftentimes, it is in the intimacy of prayer that we receive from God the seeds that will bear fruit in our lives, home, communities and nations. As apostle James said, *"The effective, fervent prayer of a righteous man avails much."*[3] In the next Chapter, we will further discuss God as our seed-giver and how we can receive and take seed from Him in order to birth His purposes on earth.

3. Worship

Worship is an attitude of the heart, which is manifested in outward expression of awe, love, trust and reverence. We are to worship and surrender our lives to God daily and involve Him in every aspect of our lives.[4] Worship is the total yielding and surrendering of self to God, in love and reverence. True worship permeates every aspect of our lives, spirit, soul and body and is not passive but active.

As Jesus said, the time has come for us to worship God in spirit and truth.[5] This means we must worship God beyond our natural senses of hearing, sight, taste, smell and touch. Worship is an expression of faith in the God we do not see, yet are willing to yield and surrender to. To worship in spirit is an attitude of the heart, and the whole heart must be engaged for worship to be acceptable to God. Worship is humanity's ultimate bond of intimacy with God. Therefore to be fruitful and multiply, we must learn to draw closer to God in worship.

4. The Holy Spirit

Jesus knew His disciples will struggle without Him so He promised to send the Holy Spirit Who would help them.[6]

Acts 1:8

"...But you shall receive power (ability, efficiency, and might) when the Holy Spirit has come upon you, and you shall be

My witnesses in Jerusalem and all Judea and Samaria and to the ends (the very bounds) of the earth."(AMP)

It is really amazing that many Christians attempt to live without the Holy Spirit! We plan and organize our lives, services and programmes without Him. We even think we can evangelise without Him! The Holy Spirit is the One Who convicts the world of sin,[7] so without His leading and involvement in our evangelistic programmes, we are bound to achieve little. He is the One Who births new souls into the kingdom,[8] yet we presume we can do without Him! It is no wonder that we are not bearing much fruitful or bringing many souls into the kingdom!

We cannot do without the Holy Spirit because He is the one Who supplies us with power, strength, grace, guidance, gifts and abilities. The Church needs these in order to be fruitful and multiply the seeds of the kingdom of God.

5. Faith

Hebrews 11:1 tells us that faith is the assurance of things hoped for and the evidence of things we have not seen. Hebrews 11:6 also says, without faith it is impossible to please God, hence, it is essential for us to cultivate a lifestyle of faith.

Hebrews 11:11-12

"By faith Sarah herself also received strength to conceive seed, and she bore a child when she was past the age, because she judged Him faithful who had promised. Therefore from one man, and him as good as dead, were born as many as the stars of the sky in multitude—

innumerable as the sand which is by the seashore"

Actually, Hebrews Chapter 11 gives a list of the heroes of faith – men and women who believed and trusted God. Sarah believed and received her child, even though she was past the menopause. If only we would stand in faith, against all odds and against what we see or hear, we will receive and we will bear fruit.

Faith in God could be likened to the turning and kicking a pregnant woman feels in her womb. Even though she has not yet seen her baby, the movement in her womb is the evidence that assures her that the foetus is alive and she will soon hold her baby in her arms. When the movement stops, everybody gets alarmed, because it means something has gone wrong or the baby has died. If our faith in God ceases, we will not possess what we desire, because without faith our fruit will not abide, as we will abort, miscarry or have stillbirths.

Spiritual Contraception

People use contraceptives to prevent themselves from getting pregnant. In the same manner, as Christians, we can stop ourselves from bearing fruit. Prophet Isaiah appealed to the women in his day against this, saying, *"Rise up, you women who are at ease. Hear my voice; you complacent daughters. In a year and some days you will be troubled, you complacent women; for the vintage will fail..."*[9]

Below is a short list of attitudes which I consider as spiritual contraceptives. We must avoid these at all costs.

- Lack of knowledge
- Lack of vision
- Unbelief
- Lack of faith
- Indifference
- Complacency

REFLECTIVE QUESTIONS

1. Review the five aids to spiritual conception. How effective are they in your own life?
2. Discuss the ways in which the 'spiritual contraceptives' could prevent a woman from being a fruitful Christian. Do any of these apply to you?
3. What other things could prevent a Christian from being fruitful?
4. What must change in your own life? Pray daily and ask God to help you.

Notes
1. Baby Hope, Online Source: http://www.babyhopes.com/articles/folic-acid.html
2. Psalm 119:49-50
3. James 5:16
4. Proverbs 3:5-6
5. John 4:22-24
6. John 14:16
7. John 16:8
8. John 3:5-7
9. Isaiah 32:9-10

Chapter Nine

THE KINGDOM-MINDED WOMAN

"For there shall the seed produce peace and prosperity; the vine shall yield her fruit and the ground shall give its increase and the heavens shall give their dew; and I will cause the remnant of this people to inherit and possess all these things."
– Zechariah 8:12 (AMP)

A New Law of Inheritance

Numbers 27:1-7

"Then the daughters of Zelophehad, the son of Hepher... son of Joseph... came near... They stood before Moses and before Eleazar the priest and before the leaders and all the congregation, at the doorway of the tent of meeting, saying, "Our father died in the wilderness, yet he was not among the company of those who gathered themselves together against the LORD in the company of Korah; but he died in his own sin, and he had no sons. Why should the name of our father be withdrawn from among his family because he had no son? Give us a possession among our father's brothers." So Moses brought their case before the LORD. Then the LORD spoke to Moses, saying, "The daughters of Zelophehad are right in their statements. You shall surely give them a hereditary possession among their father's

brothers, and you shall transfer the inheritance of their father to them."" (NASB)

This bible narrative is about five sisters, the daughters of Zelophehad, who approached Moses because they were concerned about their father's inheritance. Their father had died years before in the wilderness, and as they approached the Promised Land, these women realised that they were in danger of losing his name and inheritance. Unfortunately, they could not inherit their father's portion since the traditional practice disqualified them by maintaining that only sons could inherit.[1]

These women were concerned about their father's name and inheritance, because their father had died without a son to inherit him. Also, the absence of a son meant that there was no seed through which their father's lineage would be continued. Thus his name would be wiped out, and so would their identity! Their hope of an inheritance in the Promised Land would also be lost forever.

However, these women were not ones to be deterred! Their concern was so great that they decided to take things into their own hands and approached Moses, the priest and leaders to discuss the issue. They made their request through the proper channel, with a reference to their history. They knew their genealogy could be traced back to their forefather Joseph, for Jacob had blessed his son Joseph to be fruitful and prosperous saying,

"...By the Almighty who will bless you with blessings of heaven above, blessings of the deep that lies beneath, blessings of the breasts and of the womb. The blessings of

your father have excelled the blessings of my ancestors."[2]

Interestingly, the daughters' request was not for an inheritance previously owned by their father, as Israel had not yet reached the Promised Land. They asked for what had been promised, and as such, their request was one of great faith.

God endorsed their demand and justified it as legal, thus creating a new Inheritance Law! He said *"you shall surely give them a possession of inheritance among their father's brothers."* As a demonstration of grace, God raised these daughters to the status of sons[3] so that they could inherit their father's possessions, just as Job did for his daughters.[4]

Sons of God

Many of you reading this book can identify with the dilemma of the daughters of Zelophehad. Many of you have lost your earthly father's inheritance because you have been considered unfit to inherit due to your gender. Some of you may even have lost the inheritance of a deceased husband. This has, perhaps, affected the way you see your own inheritance in God's kingdom. Some of you are not even aware that you have an inheritance in God's kingdom because you have been taught wrongly about the things of God.

Well, once again, I have good news for you: because of the work of Calvary, God has adopted and declared us SONS and joint-heirs with Jesus Christ! Every child of God is a son of God, irrespective of their gender, and so can inherit the kingdom.

Galatians 3:26-29, 4:4-5

"For you are all <u>sons</u> of God through faith in Christ Jesus. For as many of you as were baptized into Christ have put on Christ. There is neither Jew nor Greek, there is neither slave nor free, there is neither male nor female; for you are all one in Christ Jesus. And if you are Christ's, then you are Abraham's seed, and <u>heirs</u> according to the promise ... when the fullness of the time had come, God sent forth His Son, born of a woman, born under the law, to redeem those who were under the law, that we might receive the adoption as sons."

As sons of God, the kingdom of God is our inheritance and we can rise and possess it. Indeed, we must rise and possess it! If the scriptures call us sons, we ought to behave as sons. We ought to have the attitude of sons. Sonship, in the New Testament, is not by virtue of gender, but rather is a status, position or function, which we acquire when we come into Christ. Sonship implies:

- Position and Status
- Ownership
- Authority
- Responsibility
- Preservation
- Active Participation (Work)

Like the daughters of Zelophehad, we must be concerned about our Father's name and inheritance and rise up to possess it. We must not allow God's name to be mocked, profaned or become a swear word. God's Name must be declared and passed on to the next generation! We must rise up with the same attitude as Zelophehad's daughters – bold, focused and determined – knowing what is at stake and setting our faces like flint to turn the situation around.

God's original intention was for both man and woman to rule and possess the earth and everything in it. This was lost through the Fall of Man, but regained through the death and resurrection of Christ. Hence, the responsibility of the kingdom, that is, to establish Christ's rule and reign on earth, has become ours again through Christ. The bible says that we, the saints of the Most High will receive the kingdom and will possess it forever, and the sovereignty, power and greatness of the kingdoms under the whole heaven will be handed over to us, the people of the Most High.[5] Hallelujah!

This is not an abstract and unattainable feat, but a tangible reality of our Christian faith and belief. The earth and all that is in it is ours to possess for God's kingdom glory. Bill Johnson said, *"We were born to rule… to plunder hell and establish the rule of Jesus wherever we go by preaching the gospel of the kingdom… In the original purpose of God, mankind ruled over creation. Now sin has entered the world, creation has been infected by darkness, namely, disease, sickness, afflicting spirits, poverty, natural disasters, demonic influence,* [and I will add, wars, murders, rebellion, witchcraft, rape, drug abuse and gang crimes] *etc. Our rule is still over creation, but now it is focused on exposing and undoing the works of the devil."*[6]

The Daughter's Inheritance

The story of Zelophehad's daughters did not end with God instructing Moses to give them an inheritance among their father's brothers. After a while, Moses was approached again, this time by the relatives of Zelophehad. Their concern was that if the daughters of Zelophehad married men from another tribe, their inheritance would be taken from their ancestral inheritance and added to the tribe they married into.[7]

This meant that even though the daughters had been allocated their father's inheritance, they were still in danger of losing it, and subsequently, losing his name forever. To preserve their father's inheritance, the daughters of Zelophehad had to take seed and be fruitful. However, the inheritance would be lost if they took seed from outside their own tribe. Therefore, to preserve both their father's name and inheritance, they had to take seed from the right source, as the wrong seeds would cause them to lose what they had possessed.

The Lord commanded the five daughters to choose their own husbands from within their father's tribe. This was unusual because traditionally women were not given a choice of whom to marry. The father, uncle or a male member of the family always gave a woman's hand in marriage. Yet, once again, God reinforced their status as sons by permitting them to choose their own husbands. The daughters of Zelophehad co-operated by marrying their cousins from their father's side, and their inheritance remained within their clan.

Unfortunately, many of us have taken wrong seeds and therefore, stand in danger of losing our possession in Christ.

Many of us have taken seeds of abuse, depression, oppression, and suppression. Some have taken seeds of ignorance, foolishness, jealousy, envy, slander, backbiting, anger and unforgiveness. Others have taken seeds of fear, failure, shame and guilt. Since we always multiply, incubate and birth whatever we receive and take as women, it is no surprise that many women are weak, confused, ineffective, divisive and unfruitful in the kingdom.

A pastor was having problems with some of the women leaders in his church and invited me to a meeting to discuss the issue. I sat for a while listening to the women accusing each other of not *'greeting me'*, *'being isolated'*, *'not wanting to be friends with others'*, etc. Finally, I spoke and asked them, *"Why do you attend this particular church? Do you believe that this church is where God wants you to fellowship and serve? If so, your focus must be on the vision given to your pastor and your role and responsibility in helping him to fulfil that vision. All the bickering and backbiting will cease if you focused on the church and its vision, because you will work and co-operate with each other to bring the vision to pass."* Everyone went silent! The pastor then spoke and said, *"You have spoken well! You have truly spoken like a man because this is not how women normally think!"*

Daughters of God, joint-heirs with Jesus, we stand to lose our inheritance, unless we rise up, receive and take the seeds of the kingdom and bear fruits of righteousness, peace and joy. Let us reject, abort and refuse to take any other seeds than the seeds of the kingdom. As women, it is time for us to change focus and become kingdom-minded!

Taking the Seeds of the Kingdom

Isaiah 54:5

"For your Maker is your Husband, the LORD of Hosts is His name."

So, how do we take the seeds of the kingdom? For a woman to take seed, she has to be intimate with the seed-giver. Hence to take seed from God, there has to be intimacy with Him. You cannot take seed from a distance, because seed-taking is a tactile, physical, intimate and passionate activity. If you have ever watched a rugby match, you will realise that you cannot play rugby if you don't like people touching and grabbing you. I know this example is a bit unfeminine, but, it explains the point. Naturally, you cannot take seed if you do not want to be in contact with the seed-giver. To take seed, a woman has to lie and be intimate with a man, the seed-giver. Seeds are in the loins of the seed-giver so the woman who wants to be fruitful must become one with the seed-giver.

The kingdom-minded woman, therefore, is one who is concerned about God the King's Name and inheritance. She is one who knows that the kingdom is at stake, unless she rises and takes seed. She is one who draws close to God, the King of kings, in love and intimacy, prepared to receive from Him. She places her head and ear on His heart in prayer, hearing and listening to every heartbeat and throb. She is one who is willing and prepared to draw closer to the King, to receive and take His seed. She is one who will take His seed, incubate and nurture it in her 'spiritual womb' on her knees, carry it till term (the appointed time) without giving up, and birth new life into the kingdom.

Naomi was concerned that the name of her husband and sons would be obliterated, because there was no son. Therefore, she took careful steps to rectify that. She instructed her daughter-in-law, Ruth, a Moabite woman, on what to do. Ruth was willing and co-operated with Naomi because she was also a kingdom-minded woman. Naomi chose the right seed-giver, Boaz, from within the same tribe and then she prepared Ruth to meet him. She said to Ruth:

1. Wash yourself
2. Anoint yourself
3. Put on your best garment
4. Go to the threshing floor, where your husband, the seed-giver is.

Ruth followed Naomi's instructions, married Boaz and gave birth to Obed, the father of Jesse, who was also the father of King David, from whose lineage Jesus Christ, the Messiah came.[8] Only God knows what would have happened, if Ruth had not been kingdom-minded, and prepared and positioned herself with Boaz.

Song of Solomon 2:14
"O my dove, in the clefts of the rock, in the secret place of the steep pathway, let me see your form, let me hear your voice; for your voice is sweet, and your form is lovely." (NASB)

God is calling us to intimacy so that we can receive from Him – visions, dreams, ideas, ministries, businesses, prayer burdens, etc. We must prepare ourselves and draw near to Him in intimacy. Normally, women prepare before intimacy with a man, by washing, moisturising and perfuming our bodies, and putting on the appropriate nightdress. In the same manner, like Ruth, we draw towards the Lord in intimacy, having washed (in the blood of Jesus and the word of God), anointed ourselves (in the Holy Spirit), and clothed in our garments of righteousness, at the place of prayer.

This type of preparation is what the Church, the Bride of Jesus Christ, must be engaged in as we wait for His Second Coming. The Church must be ready when He comes, and HE IS COMING SOON, perhaps sooner than we expect! The Church needs to prepare! I believe this is one of the reasons why God is raising His daughters. No one knows how to prepare a bride better than a woman. The preparation and fuss that goes on as the women and bridesmaids prepare a bride-to-be is very delightful. Thus, I believe that women will rise up and prepare the Church, the Bride of Christ, for His soon coming marriage.

Men, please do not be worried or afraid, we are not about to displace or overthrow your position. God forbid! No, we are coming with our God-given gifts, talents, abilities and strengths to join you. Together, and under the keen eye and direction of the Holy Spirit, we shall prepare the Church.

Taking the Kingdom

Matthew 11:12

"And from the days of John the Baptist until the present time, the kingdom of heaven has endured violent assault, and violent men seize it by force [as a precious prize—a share in the heavenly kingdom is sought with most ardent zeal and intense exertion]." (AMP)

What is the way forward for us? The daughters of Zelophehad, Akcah, Caleb's daughter,[9] Naomi and Ruth all possessed their inheritance because they maintained a particular attitude of ownership and responsibility. They recognised what was theirs, took the responsibility of possessing it into their own hands and moved to acquire it. They allowed nothing to hinder them – no tradition or law. They took what was rightfully theirs.

We must possess the same attitude if we are to possess the kingdom. As Jesus said, the kingdom suffers violence and can only be seized and taken by force. That instantly qualifies us. Woman, you are qualified to take the kingdom! In the natural you were designed to take seed, multiply and give birth. I don't know of any human activity or effort that is more forceful than childbirth. We can use our God-given natural reproductive qualities to take the kingdom of God. May we never have to confess, *"Our inheritance has been turned over to aliens, and our houses to foreigners."*[10]

Our present world is full of pain and panic, woe and war, turmoil and trouble. You only have to switch on your radio or television to know what is going on – terrorism, war, poverty, hunger, murder, rape, mugging, kidnapping, gang crimes, drug abuse, prostitution – the list is endless. Just a week ago, a 16 year old girl from my church was abducted and raped! As if that was not enough, the perpetuators poured acid on her! This is the world we are living in!

Jeremiah 4:31

"For I have heard a voice as of a woman in labour, the anguish as of her who brings forth her first child, the voice of the daughter of Zion bewailing herself; she spreads her hands, saying, 'Woe is me now, for my soul is weary because of murderers!'"

Lamentations 2:10-11

"Arise, cry out in the night, at the beginning of the watches; pour out your heart like water before the face of the Lord. Lift your hands toward Him for the life of your young children, who faint from hunger at the head of every street."

Woman, we can change our homes, communities, cities and nations. The solution to the world's problems lies with the Church. Jesus Christ is the solution, and He has made us the salt and light of the world. We can use our inherent strengths to bring about change.

I have in my possession a document given to me by the Bamenda Baptist Convention Women's Union, Cameroon, Central Africa. It is a five-year Plan of Activities for the Women's Union. Their first goal is to lead 105,000 children to Christ in five years! To achieve this, they have a well defined strategy, which includes training 30 Child Evangelism leaders each year, each of the 30 to train 20 Children's Ministry workers (totalling 600 workers), who will in turn lead 35 children each to the Lord every year, and disciple them! These women have appointed co-ordinators to monitor the entire action plan and have also allocated a budget for each part of their strategy! …This is just their first goal!

Other goals included ministering to widows and helping them to develop self-help activities, catering for orphans, building a Development Centre, etc. I was amazed at the women's clarity of vision, focus, commitment, drive, tenacity and love for Jesus! I truly commend them, for this is what the kingdom of God needs – ordinary women doing extraordinary things for God!

Beloved Daughter, together we can take and multiply seed, incubate and give birth by *praying and interceding and doing spiritual warfare*. We can r*aise our children and the next generation in the fear of God and the standard of His word*. We can *preach the gospel and evangelize, lead souls to Christ and disciple them when they come to the Lord*. We can *serve in the local church, teaching, leading worship, etc*. We can start *businesses to fund the gospel, feed and clothe the poor, care for orphans and widows*.

Woman, together, we can *take responsibility for the political, economic and social climates of our cities and nations, and intercede for righteousness to prevail.* Our communities can be safe again, if only we will arise! *"Peace on earth and goodwill towards men"*[12] can become a reality in our homes, communities and nations!

No One is Exempt!

Praise God that although the physical precedes the spiritual, the spiritual supersedes and exceeds the physical. Unlike the natural, no child of God should be barren or unfruitful, with regards to the things of the Spirit except by choice (briefly discussed under spiritual contraception in Chapter 8). There should also be no still miscarriages or stillbirths, unless we give up too soon or kill our dreams and visions out of impatience, ignorance and lack of faith.

I have further news for you: there is no menopausal period. We can be fruitful till we are called home or Jesus returns! Three women in the bible became fruitful in old age: Sarah, Elizabeth and Naomi (through Ruth). Through these women, God demonstrated that age does not matter if we are willing to co-operate with Him and His plans and purposes. God will always enable and use those who are willing.

On the other hand, just as it is in the natural, spiritual abortion is not an option and has no justification in the pursuit of kingdom business. In the Parable of the Talents, one of the servants refused to multiply the talent his master gave him, and like Judah's son Onan, hid it in the ground instead of investing it. This unprofitable servant incurred his master's wrath, and was thrown out into the 'outer darkness'[13] We must, therefore, employ every talent, gift, grace, ability and strength to God's service.

Isaiah 66:7-8

"Before she travailed, she brought forth; before her pain came, she gave birth to a boy." Who has heard such a

thing? Who has seen such things? Can a land be born in one day? Can a nation be brought forth all at once? As soon as Zion travailed, she also brought forth her sons." (NASB)

Yes, I know it will not be easy. I know it will take time, but, that is where women are needed once again! One of our inherent strengths is endurance. We have the ability to endure nine long months of pregnancy, accompanied by heartburns, backache and swollen feet. We can certainly go the long haul and endure the length of time it takes to bring change in our world! Unless we take the burdens, unless we carry them till term and unless we travail and labour, we will not see the change we desire, and things will deteriorate further. With the help of the Holy Spirit we can birth the fruits of righteousness and peace in our land.

Finally, WOMEN, we must arise with an ardent and passionate desire to see all of creation restored to its God-given glory, and Christ's reign and rule established on earth.[11] Together, we must work to see this fulfilled. Together, we can join the songwriter in saying, *"Thy Kingdom come, O God; Thy rule, O Christ, begin... Arise, O Morning Star, arise, and never set!"*

REFLECTION QUESTIONS

1. Look around you and prayerfully observe your home, community, city and/or nation. Are there any areas and issues of concern? Prayerfully consider the areas in which the Lord would have you focus on.

2.   Is there a burden on your heart? Usually, that is an indication of a 'seed' the Lord wants to give you, and an area in which you can serve Him. Take that 'seed' and see what God will accomplish through you.

3.   Are you still unsure? You may begin with your home and immediate community. What are the needs in the community? Ask God to show you what to do.

Notes

1.   Traditionally, only sons could inherit land and property
2.   Genesis 49:25-26
3.   The word 'them' in the Hebrew is masculine, not feminine, signifying their new status as sons.
4.   Job 42:15
5.   Daniel 7:18, 27
6.   Johnson, Bill, "When Heaven Invades Earth, A Practical Guide to a Life of Miracles", Destiny Image Publishers Inc., 2003, pg. 32
7.   Numbers 36:1-12
8.   Ruth 3:1-3
9.   Joshua 15:13-19
10.   Lamentations 5:2
11.   Isaiah 11
12.   Luke 2:14
13.   Matthew 25:14-30

Chapter Ten

MOTHER OF ALL LIVING

The name resounds from the beginning of time
A name, birthed from the loins of pain
For on that fateful day, when man fell from grace
And God pronounced judgement, not to His gain,
Adam rose and called his wife 'Chavvah'
Life-Spring and MOTHER OF ALL LIVING

What did Adam hear that day,
To give his wife such a name?
Oh, the voice of hope was so clear
For God in mercy had declared
That through the seed of Woman
Redemption shall appear.
Hope was rekindled, as God ordained
That in childbearing, woman would save the day

The trees shook at their roots
For the earth heard the voice of the Creator
It responded and took the seeds man planted.
Earth multiplied that which it received
And when it had brought forth its fruit
It earned the name Mother

Mother, every woman's desire
For ingrained in her, at the very core of her being
Is the urge to take seed and multiply
For God has created her to function as the earth,
To take seed and multiply
Bringing forth the fruit of her womb

Rachel cried, 'give me a child or I die',
Hannah knew no peace until she conceived
Sarah had given up hope,
For she considered her body dead
The Shulammite woman, Elizabeth, all received
The seed of the word and hope was alive again
At last, they too would bear that name, Mother

The miracle of birth
Is but a fusion of the divine and human.
For heaven merges with earth,
When a woman takes seed.
This is the wonder of motherhood,
That a woman would take seed, incubate and birth
Her fruit – a full blown human being.

MOTHER, such a multifaceted name
Nurturer, Nourisher, Nurse,
Life-giver, Sustainer, Protector
Strength, Grace, Solution
Mother, a song in the ear of every child,
The sweet song of the fruit of the womb
Mother, the essence of womanhood,
Worthy to be honoured and celebrated

MOTHER
A name the Church must also bear
For, indeed, she is a woman,
The wife of Christ, her bridegroom.
Not only must she bear the name
The Church must also possess the nature,
The very essence of the name.

For Mother is one who has known intimacy
Mother is one who has rejected barrenness
One who has taken seed and conceived
One who has multiplied, incubated the seed taken
And has nurtured and nourished till term
She's one who has laboured
And brought forth her fruit in pain
Mother is one who nurtures
And raises her womb's fruit, till maturity

MOTHER OF ALL LIVING...
Church, arise to Motherhood
Bride of Christ, let the cry be heard from you:
"Give me children or else I die"
Church, know no peace till you conceive
Wife of Christ, draw to your Husband in intimacy
Bride of Christ, take His seed and reproduce it
Church, nurture and nourish His seed
Church, Bride of Christ, bear fruit for your Husband...
Knowing that the hope of humanity and all creation
Lies with you arising to MOTHERHOOD

By Jennifer Wallace (Inspired by the Holy Spirit)
A Woman in Tune, Listening & Obeying
©2007